© 2021 Sami Moog

All rights reserved. No part of this publication may be reproduced, distributed, or transmitted in any form or by any means, including photocopying, recording, or other electronic or mechanical methods, without the prior written consent of the publisher, except in the case of brief quotations embodied in critical reviews and certain other noncommercial uses permitted by copyright law.

ISBN: 978-0-578-87835-5

Table of Contents

03
Salads

19
Breakfast

29
Soups

53
Entrées

101
Sides

131
Sweets

Introduction

The Fusion Cookbook is exactly that: an original collection of fusion recipes, taking flavors from all around the world. Some recipes are vegan, some are vegetarian, and others are meat-lovers' delights, but in all cases the recipes in the fusion cookbook are always made with health & well being in mind. Unlike many recipes you'll find elsewhere, these recipes are lower in fats, oils & sodium, and high in natural ingredients.

Each recipe takes flavors from at least two cuisines, oftentimes three, and combines those flavors perfectly and delicately, providing a truly unique flavor variety!

None of the recipes in this cookbook require ingredients that are difficult to find. In fact, you probably have most, if not all of the ingredients in your kitchen already. Unlike many other cookbooks which require expensive and exotic ingredients, the fusion cookbook only requires what you can find at your local grocery store.

Eat well, and live your life to the fullest!

Salads

Spicy Cauliflower Tabbouleh

A modern twist on an age-old Mediterranean salad, Spicy Cauliflower Tabbouleh is a fresh and exciting way to introduce any meal, and takes only a few minutes to make. Adding cauliflower to this time-tested recipe adds a delectable and satisfying crunch to an otherwise soft salad, adding a cruciferous zest to the eater's palate.

Recipe Serves	Preparation Time
6	10 Minutes

Ingredients	Amount	
Curly Parsley	1	Bunch
White Onion	1 1/2	Tablespoons
Chopped Tomato	1	Large
Baby Cucumber	1/2	Cup
Cauliflower, broken into pieces	1 1/2	Cups
Jalapeño	1/4	Medium
Bulgur Wheat (Dried Cracked Wheat)	1	Heaping Teaspoon
Lemon	1/2	Medium
Salt	1/2	Teaspoon
Black Pepper	1/2	Teaspoon
Cayenne Pepper	1/4	Teaspoon
Extra Virgin Olive Oil	3	Tablespoons
Carrots (optional)	2	Medium

PREPARATION

1. Chop the curly parsley to a medium coarseness – not too fine that it becomes pasty, but make sure to chop it fine enough that is can be easily east with a fork. Pro tip, if you want to be gourmet about it, remove the parsley stems and use only the leaves – the overall texture of the salad will be softer and the flavor will be richer.

2. Chop the white onion as fine as possible. An onion's flavor is sometimes difficult to manage. Too much in a single bite is overpowering, and if not evenly distributed, its flavor won't adequately disperse. Chopping the onion as fine as possible will ensure even and equal flavor distribution.

3. Chop the tomato and cucumbers and add them to the salad. As a rule of thumb, always use baby cucumbers, otherwise known as Persian cucumbers (the smaller, crunchier ones). These cucumbers are highly superior in both texture and flavor. For this salad, chop the cucumbers fine, and the tomato coarse.

4. Break apart the cauliflower into its naturally forming pieces, and size according to your own preference, and add to the mix.

5. Add the heaping teaspoon of cracked wheat, also called bulgur wheat. This can

SPICY CAULIFLOWER TABBOULEH

be purchased in most grocery stores, and certainly in all Mediterranean stores. The wheat adds bulk to the salad, and subtle flavor. Don't overlook this ingredient!

6. Chop the jalapeño fine, and add it to the mix. Note that every jalapeño has a different spice intensity, so measure according to your ability to handle spice.

7. Add the dressing (lemon, salt, black pepper, cayenne pepper, and extra virgin olive oil). Pro tip: If you are preparing the salad but eating/serving it later, don't add the salt just yet. Salt causes salads to become soggy if left to sit for a while.

Lentil Salad

This salad doubles as a main course, due to its overload of fiber, protein and key vitamins & minerals. The key ingredient here is green apple, which accentuates the brown lentils beautifully! Whether post-workout, or as a side dish on Thanksgiving, this salad is as unique as it is nutritious.

Recipe Serves	Cook Time
6	40 minutes

Ingredients	Amount	
Whole Brown Lentils	1	Cup
Cilantro	1/2	Bunch
Tomato	1	Large
Baby Cucumber	2	Small
White Onion, chopped	2	Tablespoons
Green Apple	1	Large
Jalapeño	1/2	Medium
Lemon	1/2	Medium
Salt	1/2	Teaspoon
Extra Virgin Olive Oil	2	Tablespoons
Black Pepper	1/4	Teaspoon
Cumin	1/2	Teaspoon
Pomegranate (optional)	1/4	Cup

Preparation

1. Rinse plain, brown lentils in a strainer. Make sure the lentils are whole, not split.

2. Place in a pot and cover with water and bring to a boil. Reduce heat to medium-low and simmer for approximately 20 minutes, or until soft. The lentils, when fully cooked, should not break apart. Each lentil should remain intact but should be soft when chewed.

3. As the lentils cook, they will absorb water. Periodically cover with water and allow to continue cooking. When the lentils are finished, strain and set aside to cool to room temperature.

   Note: do not place in the fridge to cool faster — this will ruin the texture!

4. While the lentils are cooking, dice your jalapeño, green apple, tomato, and onion into small pieces. Only a small amount of onion is called for in this recipe – don't overdo it! Green string onion is a fine substitute to white onion if you prefer that flavor.

5. Chop the cilantro, using only the leaves and not the stems. The cilantro should be chopped coarse, not fine.

Lentil Salad

6. If you are including the optional pomegranate, break apart the rubies into individual pieces, and add to the prepared vegetables.

7. Once the lentils are cooled to room temperature, add all of the ingredients together.

8. Season with lemon, salt, extra virgin olive oil, cumin, and black pepper. Mix well, and place in the fridge to reach a cool temperature, and enjoy!

Lebanese-Greek Salad

A grand mixture of Greek and Lebanese flavors, this salad is as refreshing as it is colorful! The feta accentuates the olives perfectly, as does the irresistible crunch of the carrots blend perfectly with the savory cherry tomatoes. This salad is as healthy as it is delicious!

Recipe Serves	Preparation Time
5	15 Minutes

Ingredients	Amount	
Romaine Lettuce	1	Large Head
Cherry Tomatoes	10	Tomatoes
Green Olives	10	Olives
Baby Cucumber	2	Medium
Carrot	1	Stalk
White Onion, chopped	1	Tablespoon
Feta Cheese	1/4	Cup
Jalapeño	1/4	Medium
Parsley	1/4	Bunch
Lemon	1/2	Medium
Extra Virgin Olive Oil	2	Tablespoons
Black Pepper	1/4	Teaspoon
Salt	1/4	Teaspoon

PREPARATION

1. Chop the romaine lettuce into small pieces, and slice the cherry tomatoes in half, lengthwise.

2. Remove the seeds from each olive and cut each olive once or twice. Make sure to remove the seeds and toss them aside, so that the stone seeds don't accidentally fall into the salad.

3. Chop the onion as finely as possible. The smaller the onion pieces, the more delicate their flavor will be.

4. Chop, or alternatively, grate the carrot, and dice the cucumbers.

5. Chop the jalapeño in large pieces. With this salad, you don't want any individual bite to contain jalapeño, but you want the spice to disperse throughout.

6. Dice the parsley bunch, removing the stems for a softer, more delicate texture.

7. Crumble the feta cheese. For this salad, Bulgarian feta is

LEBANESE-GREEK SALAD

recommended, as opposed to the other main type of feta, French. Bulgarian feta is more sour, and less creamy than its French counterpart.

8. Season the salad with the juice of half a lemon, a couple tablespoons of extra virgin olive oil, black pepper and salt.

The Everything Salad

A cross between Mediterranean and Western salad styles, The Everything Salad is something anyone who enjoys fresh greens is bound to enjoy! The special ingredient in this salad is jalapeño – yes, spicy salad. It may take a little bravery to try it, but once you taste it you'll find yourself putting jalapeños in plenty of salad varieties!

Recipe Serves	Preparation Time	
6	10 Minutes	
Ingredients	**Amount**	
Curly Parsley	1	Bunch
White Onion	1 1/2	Tablespoons
Chopped Tomato	1	Large
Baby Cucumber	1/2	Cup
Cauliflower, broken into pieces	1 1/2	Cups
Jalapeño	1/4	Medium
Bulgur Wheat (Dried Cracked Wheat)	1	Heaping Teaspoon
Avocado	1	Medium
Red Bell Pepper	1/2	Medium
Carrots	2	Stalks
Lemon	1/2	Medium
Salt	1/2	Teaspoon
Black Pepper	1/2	Teaspoon
Cayenne Pepper	1/4	Teaspoon
Extra Virgin Olive Oil	3	Tablespoons

Preparation

1. Chop parsley and white onion very fine. Remove the stems for a softer texture.

2. Chop tomato, cucumber, avocado, jalapeño, red bell pepper, and carrots, into small pieces. Break apart cauliflower into natural smaller pieces.

3. Add a heaping spoon of cracked wheat.

4. Season with lemon, extra virgin olive oil, black pepper, cayenne pepper, and salt. Lemon can be substituted with apple cider vinegar, according to preference.

THE EVERYTHING SALAD

5. Mix everything together and enjoy!

Tuna Salad

Do salads have to be vegan? Not always, and this tuna salad is as healthy and delicious as can be. It's the celery leaves: they're the key ingredient, filing the entire salad with a beautifully bitter flavor. The avocado moistens the otherwise dry tuna, and the vegetable medley make this salad a true rainbow of color.

Recipe Serves	Preparation Time	
4	10 Minutes	

Ingredients	Amount	
Tuna	1	Can
Celery	2	Stalks
Celery Leaves	1	Bunch
Tomato	1	Medium
Baby Cucumber	2	Small
Red Bell Pepper	1/2	Large
Red Bell Pepper Seeds	1	Tablespoon
Jalapeño	1/4	Medium
Broccoli	1/4	Crown
Parsley	1/2	Bunch
Avocado	1/2	Small
Lemon	1/2	Medium
Extra Virgin Olive Oil	2	Tablespoons
Salt	1/2	Teaspoon
Black Pepper	1/4	Teaspoon
Paprika	1/4	Teaspoon
Cayenne Pepper	1/4	Teaspoon

Preparation

1. Open a can of tuna and rinse with water in a strainer, and break apart into small pieces. Place in large salad bowl.

2. For this salad, all of the vegetables should be chopped as finely as possible.

3. Chop the parsley, removing the stems if you want the salad to have a softer texture, though this isn't necessary. Slice half a red bell pepper horizontally and dice into small pieces. Gather all seeds, which usually equates to a full tablespoon if using a mature pepper. Throw those seeds into the salad bowl, along with the parsley and chopped pepper.

4. Get a celery bunch, and take 1-2 stalks and slice them. Then, break apart the celery bunch so that you can gather the interior stalks – the soft, light-green ones with the leaves on top, and slice those as well, making sure to include all of the light-colored leaves on top. Throw that into the salad bowl.

5. Dice the jalapeño, tomato and cucumbers. Note that like all salad recipes in The Fusion Cookbook, when cucumbers are mentioned, and especially when multiple cucumbers are included, baby cucumbers, otherwise known as Persian cucumbers, are the recommended variety. These cucumbers are very small, crunchy and bursting with flavor. Their texture, crunch and flavor are unmatched relative to other cucumber varieties. Throw them into the salad bowl.

6. Break apart the broccoli into its smallest possible natural pieces and toss them in the bowl.

7. Dice half an avocado. Pro tip: when dicing avocado (or any vegetable), cut diagonally. The diamond shape will be more visually pleasing.

8. Season the salad with lemon, extra virgin olive oil, salt, black pepper, and cayenne pepper. Cayenne pepper is optional, as is the jalapeño. If you don't like a spicy salad then disregard those ingredients.

9. Apple cider vinegar is a perfectly suitable alternative to lemon. Note that canned tuna is a dry meat, and so more oil may be necessary to ensure a smooth texture. Taste before serving, and slowly add a tiny amount at a time until the overall salad texture is perfect. Serve alone or with you favorite crackers and enjoy!

Tuna Salad

Mint Salad

Another non-vegan salad, this delicious fusion salad incorporates Bulgarian feta cheese with beets and other delicious vegetables. Healthy, hearty, and especially minty, this salad's key ingredient is peppermint leaves, which adds a burst of refreshment to the palate!

Recipe Serves	Preparation Time
2	10 Minutes

Ingredients	Amount	
Cauliflower	1/4	Medium
Parsley	1/2	Bunch
Mint Leaves	1/2	Bunch
Cherry Tomatoes	10	Medium
Persian Cucumber	1	Medium
Feta Cheese	1/4	Cup
Carrot	1	Medium
Beets	1	Medium
Lemon	1/2	Medium
Olive	2	Tablespoons
Salt	1/2	Teaspoon
Chili Flakes	1/4	Teaspoon

Preparation

1. Wash & rinse the parsley and mint leaves, then chop and place into a salad bowl.

2. Wash & rinse the cherry tomatoes and Persian cucumber and place in the salad bowl.

3. Peel the carrot, and chop and add to the medley.

4. Break apart the feta cheese and add to the bowl. There are two main types of feta cheese: Bulgarian and French. Bulgarian is more sour and dry, while French is heavier and creamier. Both will work for this salad, but Bulgarian is recommended.

5. Chop the beet and add to the salad. Please note that the beet must be cooked and cooled. Most grocery stores sell ready-to-eat beets.

Mint Salad

6. Break apart the cauliflower into small, natural pieces and add to the salad.

7. Squeeze the lemon, and add to the salad along with the olive oil, salt, and chili flakes

8. Mix well, and enjoy!

Tuna & Beet Salad

Another tuna salad, this one is naturally sweetened with beets. A delicious blend of tuna, cruciferous and beet flavors, this fusion salad offers a unique blend of soft and crunchy textures!

Recipe Serves	Preparation Time
2	10 Minutes

Ingredients	Amount	
Tuna	1	Can
Broccoli	1/4	Crown
Carrots	1	Medium
Cherry Tomatoes	10	Medium
Celery	2	Stalks
Beets	1	Medium
Mint Leaves	2	Stems
Persian Cucumber	1	Medium
Lemon	1/2	Medium
Olive	2	Tablespoons
Salt	1/2	Teaspoon

Preparation

1. Break apart and rinse the broccoli, and place in a salad bowl.

2. Wash & rinse the cherry tomatoes, celery and Persian cucumber, chop, and place in the salad bowl

3. Peel the carrot, and chop and add to the medley.

4. Chop the beet and add to the salad. Please note that the beet must be cooked and cooled. Most grocery stores sell ready-to-eat beets.

5. Remove the mint leaves from the stems, chop coarsely and add to the salad bowl.

6. Squeeze the lemon, and add to the salad along with the olive oil, and salt.

7. Mix well, and enjoy!

TUNA & BEET SALAD

Breakfast

SCRAMBLED EGGS WITH VEGETABLES

Green eggs & ham is so retro – this recipe will land you a plate of pink eggs! (Ham not included). Taking a Mediterranean twist on a classic breakfast staple, these eggs are slightly sweet due to the red bell pepper, and slightly sour due to the tomato. The flavor ends up balancing perfectly for a wholesome, nutritious meal!

Recipe Serves		Cook Time	
2		10 Minutes	

Ingredients	Amount	
Eggs	4	Large
Tomato	1	Small
Cilantro	2	Tablespoons
Red Bell Pepper	1 1/2	Tablespoons
Green Bell Pepper	2	Tablespoons
Salt	1/2	Teaspoon
Black Pepper	1/4	Teaspoon
Extra Virgin Olive Oil	2	Tablespoons
Bread (optional)		

Preparation

1. Chop the cilantro fine and chop the red bell pepper & tomato into very small pieces.

2. Heat extra virgin olive in a pan and add the vegetables to sauté on medium heat for 2 minutes.

3. Crack the eggs over the pan and mix all the ingredients together. Continue mixing throughout the cooking process, which should take about 5 minutes.

4. The color of the eggs will become a strawberry pink, and the eggs are ready to serve!

5. Enjoy with your choice of bread!

Scrambled Eggs With Vegetables

Oatmeal

A classic breakfast staple, this oatmeal is absolutely dazzling any time of day, with its pumpkin and vanilla flavors complementing the natural fruit flavors of apples and raisins. This oatmeal is an upgraded version of the classic meal we all love!

Recipe Serves	Cook Time
3	10 Minutes

Ingredients	Amount	
Rolled Oats (Oatmeal)	1	Cup
Water (or Milk)	2	Cups
Raisins	1/4	Cup
Red Apple	1	Small
Dried Fruit of Your Choice	2	Tablespoons
Sugar	1 1/2	Tablespoons
Vanilla Extract	1	Teaspoon
Pumpkin Spice	1/2	Teaspoon
Cinnamon	1	Teaspoon
Salt	1/4	Teaspoon

Preparation

1. Dice a red apple into small pieces, sprinkle with cinnamon, and set aside. Apples may be peeled, or with skin, depending on personal preference.

2. Pour a cup of oats in a pot and cover with 2 cups of milk or water.

3. Add seasoning to oatmeal: cinnamon, salt, sugar, vanilla extract, and pumpkin spice. Stir very well.

4. Bring to a boil, then simmer over low heat for 3 minutes.

5. Add diced apples to pot and continue simmering for 3 minutes.

6. When oatmeal is soft and fully cooked, remove from pot and place in a bowl, and mix in raising and any other dried fruit of your choice.

OATMEAL

EGG & BELL PEPPER RINGS

These egg flats will catch the eye of anyone who glances at them. Perfectly contained within bell pepper rings, and filled with green and red colors from the cilantro and bell peppers, this egg dish will wow the palate as much as it wows the eyes.

Recipe Serves	Cook Time
4	10 Minutes

Ingredients	Amount	
Eggs	4	Large
Green Bell Pepper	2	Slices
Red Bell Pepper	2	Slices
Cilantro, chopped	1/4	Bunch
Tomato	1/2	Large
Salt	1/2	Teaspoon
Black Pepper	1/2	Teaspoon
Green & Red Bell Peppers, chopped	1/4	Cup
Grapeseed Oil (or corn oil)	3	Tablespoons
Bread (optional)		

Preparation

1. Slice a red & green bell pepper horizontally and set aside. Chop remainder of bell peppers into small pieces.

2. Finely chop cilantro and tomato into small pieces.

3. Place cilantro, tomato and chopped bell peppers into a bowl and mix.

4. Crack 4 eggs into bowl of vegetables and mix evenly, and season with salt and black pepper.

5. In a pan, heat grapeseed oil. Corn oil is a perfectly fine substitute.

6. When oil is heated, place bell pepper rings onto the pan, and pour a small amount of egg mixture into each ring, filled to the top. Eggs will leak from under the bell pepper rings – that's ok.

EGG & BELL PEPPER RINGS

7. Once eggs are cooked, use a spatula to separate the 4 egg-bell pepper pancakes, and flip to evenly cook both sides.

8. Once eggs are fully cooked on both sides, serve with your favorite bread, and enjoy!

Sunny Side Up Eggs in Pepper Rings

This ultra-presentable breakfast is colorful, delicious and easy to make! Perfectly encased within green & red bell pepper rings, these eggs sunny side up will have you walking on sunshine all day!

Recipe Serves	Cook Time
4	10 Minutes

Ingredients	Amount	
Eggs	4	Large
Red Bell Pepper	2	Sliced Rings
Green Bell Pepper	2	Sliced Rings
Bell Pepper Seeds	1	Teaspoon
Corn Oil	4	Tablespoons
Salt	1/4	Teaspoon
Black Pepper	1/4	Teaspoon
Jalapeño (optional)	1/4	Small
Bread (optional)		

Preparation

1. Slice your bell peppers horizontally into rings. Cut a single ring for each egg.

2. Remove the seeds from inside the bell peppers and save for later.

3. Chop the optional jalapeño into small pieces and save for later.

4. In a pan, heat the corn oil under medium heat and when sufficiently hot, place the rings on the pan, and crack the eggs – one in each ring. Be sure not to break the yolk.

5. Some of the egg white will seep from underneath the pepper rings – this is normal. If too much leaks, your oil wasn't hot enough. However, some amount will leak and that's ok. Just allow it to cook naturally and then cut it away with your spatula.

6. Continuously spoon the sizzling oil over the eggs to cook them sunny side up.

7. Once the eggs are cooked, with your spatula remove them from the pan and onto your serving plate. Do not flip (unless you want to cook your eggs over easy/medium/hard). However, this recipe calls for cooking them sunny side up.

8. On your serving plate, sprinkle the bell pepper seeds and the finely chopped jalapeño over the eggs, and serve with bread of your choice!

Sunny Side Up Eggs in Pepper Rings

Soups

Chickpea Soup

This soup is a protein packed, vegan friendly, and highly versatile dish that serves as soup, pasta sauce, or a delightful dipping sauce for chicken tenders! Jam packed with protein, this soup makes a great pre- or post-workout meal. Soothing to the digestive system, the chickpeas will help you feel fuller for longer with their abundance of fiber.

Recipe Serves	Cook Time
4	45 Minutes

Ingredients	Amount	
Chickpeas, cooked	2	Cups
White Onion	1/3	Onion
Chopped Tomato	2/3	Large
Garlic, crushed	1	Clove
Extra Virgin Olive Oil	2	Tablespoons
Sesame Seeds	1	Teaspoon
Salt	1/2	Teaspoon
Black Pepper	1/4	Teaspoon
Cumin	1/2	Teaspoon
Paprika	1/2	Teaspoon
Sage	1/3	Teaspoon
Cayenne Pepper	1/4	Teaspoon

PREPARATION

1. Crush the clove of garlic. Pro tip: when you crush garlic, make sure to let it sit for 10–15 minutes before cooking. Studies have shown that certain enzymes are activated with oxygen, upon slicing or crushing garlic, which cause certain healthy compounds to become heat resistant, thereby preserving garlic's health effects throughout the cooking process. These enzymes take roughly 10-15 minutes to fully activate.

2. Chop the white onion as fine as possible.

3. Chop the tomato into small pieces.

4. Sauté the garlic and onion over medium heat in olive oil, stirring continuously to prevent browning or burning.

5. While sautéing the garlic and onion, add the seasoning (salt, black pepper, cumin, paprika, cayenne pepper, and sesame seeds. Continue stirring continuously until the onion begins to turn slightly brown.

6. Add the chopped tomato and continue stirring, for another minute or so, then add the chickpeas and stir to even mix all the ingredients. Canned chickpeas may be added as is; dried chickpeas must be cooked first.

7. Add enough water to cover all ingredients by half an inch and stir.

CHICKPEA SOUP

8. Turn heat to medium-low, place cover over pot, and allow to simmer for 45 minutes, periodically stirring.

9. At approximately 30 minutes into simmering, use a whisk or a potato masher and mash the soup until all chickpeas are completely mashed. Add water according to desired thickness, or do not add water if you prefer a thicker soup. Continue stirring for another 15 minutes and the soup will be ready to serve.

Vegetable Soup

The ultimate vegetable soup! This incredible soup is bursting with flavor, and the spicy aroma will have your sinuses opening before the soup is even served! This recipe is vegan friendly, incredibly easy to make, and totally delicious!

Recipe Serves	Cook Time
5	45 Minutes

Ingredients	Amount	
Mushrooms	1	Box
Onion	1	Medium
Peas	1/2	Cup
Corn	1/2	Cup
Green Bell Pepper	1	Large
Tomatoes	3	Medium
Carrots	2	Stalks
Potato	1	Medium
Zucchini	1	Medium
Squash	1	Small
Spinach	1/4	Cup
Jalapeño	1	Small
Tomato Sauce	3	Tablespoons
Extra Virgin Olive Oil	2	Tablespoons
Water	6 1/2	Cups
Salt	1	Tablespoon
Paprika	1	Teaspoon
Black Pepper	1/2	Teaspoon

Preparation

1. Wash and rinse all of the vegetables, and dice to a medium coarseness. As a general rule, for this soup, all the ingredients should be diced to roughly the same size, except the onion. Mince the onion into very fine pieces. If you are using fresh spinach, mince fine as well. If you are using frozen chopped spinach, set aside for now.

2. Once all the vegetables have been diced and minced, place in a bowl and set aside. If you are using frozen corn & peas, keep those aside as well. If fresh, add to vegetable medley.

3. Bring water to a boil on high heat in a large cooking pot.

4. When the water is boiling, add all the ingredients, including the tomato sauce and seasoning.

5. Mix soup very thoroughly.

6. Keep on high heat and bring soup to a boil, stirring frequently.

Vegetable Soup

7. When water has reached a boil, reduce heat to low, place lid on the pot, and simmer for 40 minutes, stirring occasionally.

Hearty Cauliflower & Lentil Bow-Tie Soup

An intensely hearty soup, this fiber and nutrient packed soup will keep you full all day long! Rich and thick, cauliflower and mashed carrots, with lentils and cracked wheat, create the broth, with several complimentary flavors working in tandem to provide what may be the most delicious soup you've ever had!

Recipe Serves	Cook Time
4	60 Minutes

Ingredients	Amount	
Garlic, crushed	1	Clove
White Onion	1/2	Medium
Butter	1/2	Teaspoon
Cracked Wheat (Bulgur Wheat)	3	Tablespoons
Red Lentils	3	Teaspoons
Cauliflower	1/4	Large
Carrots	3	Medium
Potato	1	Medium
Bow-Tie Pasta (Farfalle)	1/4	Cup
Salt	1/2	Teaspoon
Black Pepper	1/4	Teaspoon

Preparation

1. Bring water to a boil in a smaller, separate pot from the main cooking pot. Keep on high heat.

2. Crush the clove of garlic, and finely chop the onion.

3. Peel and chop the potato, and leave on the side.

4. Rinse the bulgur wheat and red lentils in a strainer.

5. Peel and coarsely chop the carrots, and break apart the cauliflower into natural pieces. Add the carrots to the smaller pot of boiling water. Let the carrots boil for 20 minutes, then add the cauliflower and boil together for another 20 minutes, then strain and place in a bowl.

6. Melt the butter in a pot under medium heat. Alternatively, you may use corn oil, grapeseed oil, or avocado oil.

7. Sauté the garlic and onions in the pot, stirring continuously to prevent browning. After a few minutes, add water and bring to a boil. Add the salt and black pepper. From start to finish, this pot should cook on medium heat with the lid on for 60 minutes on medium heat, stirring occasionally. Adding water may be necessary as water evaporates.

8. When the main pot has come to a boil, let boil on medium for 10 minutes, then add the red lentils and cracked wheat.15

Hearty Cauliflower & Lentil Bow-Tie Soup

minutes later, add the chopped potato. Let simmer on medium heat with lid on.

9. 10 minutes after adding the potato, add the bow-tie pasta. Continue to cook on medium heat, stirring occasionally.

10. Strain the carrots and cauliflower and put in a bowl. Using a potato masher or something similar, mash together until the carrots and cauliflower form a paste. Add to the main pot of soup, and continue to boil soup for another 10 minutes, stirring frequently.

11. Serve, and enjoy!

Cauliflower & Chicken Soup

This protein-packed soup is great by itself or as a side dish to a main course! With the rich flavor form the chicken, and the savory aroma of the boiled cauliflower, this soup serves as a hearty & unique soup for any season!

Recipe Serves	Cook Time
4	60 Minutes

Ingredients	Amount	
Garlic, crushed	1	Clove
White Onion	1/2	Medium
Butter	1/2	Teaspoon
Cracked Wheat (Bulgur Wheat)	3	Tablespoons
Chicken Breast	1	Breast
Cauliflower	1/4	Large
Sage	1	Teaspoon
Salt	1/2	Teaspoon
Black Pepper	3/4	Teaspoon

Preparation

1. Crush the clove of garlic and finely chop the onion.

2. Melt the butter in a pot and sauté the garlic and onion, stirring continuously to precent burning.

3. Fill the pot with water and bring to a boil and simmer on medium heat for 30 minutes.

4. Chop the chicken breast into small pieces and marinate with sage and black pepper.

5. Add the cracked wheat and chicken to the pot, bring to a boil then simmer on medium heat for 20-30 minutes, depending on the size of the chicken pieces.

6. While the chicken cooks, bring water to a boil in another pot and add the cauliflower. Boil on high heat for 20 minutes, then strain and place in a bowl.

7. Mash the cauliflower until it forms a paste, and add to the main cooking pot and stir well.

8. Continue cooking on medium-low for 10 more minutes, then serve & enjoy!

Cauliflower & Chicken Soup

Chicken Noodle Soup

One of the most popular soups, this chicken noodle recipe will ignite all your senses. From crunchy peas and corn to smooth Mafalda noodles, this soup is great any time of year!

Recipe Serves	Cook Time	
4	45 Minutes	
Ingredients	**Amount**	
Chicken Breast	1	Medium
Garlic	1	Clove
Onion	1/2	Medium
Jasmine Rice	1/4	Cup
Pasta (Mafalda Noodles)	3/4	Cup
Carrots	1	Medium
Peas	1/4	Cup
Corn	1/4	Cup
Spinach	1/4	Cup
Salt	1/2	Teaspoon
Black Pepper	1/4	Teaspoon
Olive Oil	1	Teaspoon
Optional Lemon	1/2	Medium
Optional Celery	1	Stalk

Preparation

1. Crush the garlic and finely chop the onion.

2. Cut the chicken breast into small or medium pieces.

3. Add olive oil to a cooking pot and sauté the chicken, onion and garlic, salt, and black pepper until the chicken is cooked on the outside, then fill the pot with water and bring to a boil.

4. Simmer on medium-low heat with the lid on for 10 minutes, stirring occasionally.

5. Add the jasmine rice and chopped carrot and let simmer for another 10 minutes.

Chicken Noodle Soup

6. Add the pasta, frozen corn, peas and chopped spinach, and cook for 15 minutes. For this soup, use Mafalda noodles. If adding the optional celery, add now as well. The celery should be finely sliced.

7. When serving, add optional squeezed lemon.

Hearty Lentil Soup

Not for those who have been snacking all day, this dish is incredibly filling, so come to dinner hungry! A naturally thick soup, it can probably be described more as a stew. Heavy on the stomach, and filling as can be, this hearty lentil soup is a great way to end the evening before turning in for the night!

Recipe Serves	Cook Time
4	45 Minutes

Ingredients	Amount	
Red Split Lentils	1/2	Cup
Potato	1	Medium
Cauliflower	1/4	Head
Peas	1/4	Cup
Corn	1/4	Cup
Jasmine Rice	1/4	Cup
Turmeric	1	Teaspoon
Garlic, Crushed	1	Clove
Ginger, crushed	1	Teaspoon
Basil, chopped	1	Teaspoon
Sage	1/2	Teaspoon
Salt	1/2	Teaspoon
Chicken Breast (optional)	1	Breast
Grapeseed Oil	1	Tablespoon

Preparation

1. Crush the garlic and ginger together, chop a few basil leaves and mix together.

2. Dice the potato into small cubes and break apart the cauliflower into medium sized pieces.

3. This soup can be vegan or made with chicken breast. If choosing to go with chicken breast, slice the breast into medium sized strips and season with turmeric, the ginger, basil & garlic mixture, and sage. Sauté the ginger in cooking oil until golden brown. If choosing to make this soup vegan, simply add the seasoning to the ginger, garlic & basil mix and sauté that in cooking oil for a minute on low heat.

4. Rinse the red lentils and jasmine rice under running water, separately, and add the red lentils. Let cook for 15 minutes and then add the jasmine rice

Hearty Lentil Soup

and potatoes. Let cook for 20 minutes.

5. As you cook this soup, it will become thicker and thicker. You can add water to preference, but this soup is meant to be served not as a watery broth but as a thick, hearty stew.

6. Add the peas and let cook for 5 minutes, and then add the corn and cauliflower and cook for 5-7 minutes.

7. Serve, and enjoy!

Cumin & Lentil Soup

Smooth & silky, this bright yellow soup will fill you with an incredible sense of satiety. Upbeat in color and flavor, this cumin & lentil soup is perfect for bringing with you in a thermos or eating out of a bowl at home. Kind of spicy, kind of savory, this soup has a delightful fusion of flavors.

Recipe Serves	Cook Time
6	60 Minutes

Ingredients	Amount	
Red Split Lentils	1	Cup
Yellow Onion	1/2	Large
Cumin	2	Tablespoons
Salt	1/2	Teaspoon
Black Pepper	1/4	Teaspoon
Cilantro	3-4	Stems
Corn Oil	1	Tablespoon
Jalapeño (optional)	1	Medium

PREPARATION

1. Rinse the cup of red split lentils under running water.

2. Cut the half-onion into several medium sized chunks. These don't have to be diced any further, as they will melt into the broth.

3. Cut the jalapeño (optional) into several small pieces.

4. Heat the corn oil in a pot, then toss in the onion and jalapeño. Briefly sauté the two ingredients for a minute or so, stirring frequently.

5. While sautéing, season the onion and jalapeño with cumin, salt and black pepper.

6. Add the cup of red lentils, and stir thoroughly, and immediately add water, covering the ingredients by an inch or so.

7. Bring to a boil, then reduce the heat to medium and allow to simmer for one hour, stirring frequently.

8. When the soup is nearly finished, remove the leaves from a few stems of cilantro, clean them, and place them in the pot and continue cooking for 5 more minutes.

9. When you pour the soup into a bowl, pour through a strainer to ensure the soup is silky smooth. When ready, the soup should be a uniform, yellow, thick broth.

CUMIN & LENTIL SOUP

Indian-Thai Soup

If you like the spice Indian cuisine offers, and the savory flavor Thai food offers, this soup is the way to go! Hearty and chunky, this soup is half soup and half stew, and will definitely add aroma and variety to any dinner table.

Recipe Serves	Cook Time	
4	60 Minutes	
Ingredients	**Amount**	
White Onion	1/4	Large
Jasmine Rice	1/3	Cup
Red Split Lentils	1/2	Cup
Cauliflower	1/2	Crown
Potato	1	Medium
Basil, chopped	1	Teaspoon
Turmeric	1	Heaping Tablespoon
Cumin	2	Tablespoons
Salt	1/2	Teaspoon
Chili Flakes	1/2	Teaspoon
Sage	1	Teaspoon
Oregano	1/4	Teaspoon
Grapeseed Oil	1	Tablespooon

Preparation

1. Dice the onion into small pieces.

2. Heat the grapeseed oil in a cooking pot and when hot, add the diced onion.

3. While the onion is sautéing, season generously with turmeric, cumin, chili flakes & oregano, and continue stirring and sautéing.

4. When the onion has turned golden brown, fill the pot with water and bring to a boil.

5. Place the red lentils and jasmine rice in the boiling water, and season the broth with sage, basil and salt.

6. Simmer on medium heat for 10 minutes, then add the potatoes, and continue cooking for 20 minutes, stirring occasionally. More water may need to be added as the jasmine rice and red lentils absorb. Add more or not, depending on how thick you desire the soup to be.

7. Break apart the cauliflower into medium size pieces and add to the soup. Bring to a boil, and continue simmering for another 10 minutes, stirring occasionally.

INDIAN-THAI SOUP

Spinach and Red Potato Soup

Classic American meets old world spice, this soup blends hearty red potatoes with European and Mediterranean spices, creating a delectable fusion balanced very well on the palate! Not spicy by nature, this herb-filled soup will warm the body as it fills the belly.

Recipe Serves	Cook Time
3	50 Minutes

Ingredients	Amount	
Mini Red Potatoes	5	Small
Red Split Lentils	1/4	Cup
Jasmine Rice	1/4	Cup
Garlic	1	Clove
Spinach, chopped	1/2	Cup
Broccoli	1/3	Crown
Corn	1/4	Cup
Celery, Including Leaves	2	Stalks
Turmeric	1	Teaspoon
Ginger, crushed	1/4	Tablespoon
Oregano	1	Teaspoon
Basil	1	Teaspoon
Sage	1/2	Teaspoon
Salt	1/2	Teaspoon
Extra Virgin Olive Oil	1	Tablespoon

PREPARATION

1. Wash and slice the red potatoes in half.

2. Crush a clove of garlic and twice that amount of ginger, and mix together. Mix together with basil, sage, turmeric, oregano, and salt.

3. Heat extra virgin olive oil in a pot and sauté potatoes with garlic, ginger & seasoning mixture for 1 minute on low heat.

4. Rinse the red lentils and jasmine rice in a strainer, then fill your pot with water and bring to a boil, and add the red lentils and jasmine rice, then simmer on medium heat for 50 minutes, covered, stirring occasionally.

5. Wash and chop 2-3 celery stalks. Use the inner stalks, with the leaves intact. These inner stalks hold a different texture and flavor to the outer stalks, and for this soup only the inner stalks should be used.

SPINACH AND RED POTATO SOUP

6. After the soup has been simmering for 30 minutes, add the celery, corn, and chopped spinach. Bring to a boil then continue simmering. Stir well.

7. 10 minutes later, add the broccoli heads, bring to a boil and continue simmering for 10 minutes.

8. Serve, and enjoy!

Bean & Vegetable Soup

Filling, vegetarian & bursting with flavor, don't let the thin broth confuse you! This soup is as filling as it is healthy! A combination of Mediterranean and American ingredients, and a combination of beans and vegetables, this fusion soup is great as a starter or a compliment to an entrée!

Recipe Serves	Cook Time
2	60 Minutes

Ingredients	Amount	
Chickpeas	1 1/2	Cups
Lima Beans	1/4	Cup
Red Bell Pepper	1/2	Medium
Corn	1/4	Cup
Peas	1/4	Cup
Red Lentils	1	Tablespoon
Cauliflower	1/4	Medium
Cracked Wheat	2	Teaspoons
Sesame Seeds	1	Teaspoon
Basil	1/2	Teaspoon
Sage	1/2	Teaspoon
Garlic	1	Clove
Onion	1/4	Medium
Olive Oil	2	Teaspoons

Preparation

1. *Crush the garlic and finely chop the onion and red bell pepper.*

2. *In a pot, pour the olive oil and heat over medium heat. Add the onion, garlic and red bell pepper, basil and sage, and sauté.*

3. *Add water to the pot and bring to a boil. Place lid over pot and cook on medium heat for 15 minutes minutes, stirring occasionally.*

4. *Add the lentils, sesame seeds, and cracked wheat, stir, and place lid back on the pot. Continue cooking for 20 more minutes, stirring occasionally.*

5. *Add the chickpeas and lima beans. Canned chickpeas may be strained and added as is. Dry chickpeas must be cooked first. Continue cooking for 10 minutes.*

6. *Add the corn, peas, cauliflower, and continue cooking for another 10 to 15 minutes, depending how soft you like the cauliflower.*

7. *Serve & enjoy!*

Bean & Vegetable Soup

49

Pea Broth Soup

This soup, when finished and ready to serve, will likely look like something out of a comic book, with its striking lime green color, but fear not! It is incredibly tasty and light on the palate. With peas as the core ingredient, this watery soup is great to have any day of the week.

Recipe Serves	Cook Time
4	45 Minutes

Ingredients	Amount	
Peas	1	Cup
Celery	2	Stalks
Broccoli	1/4	Crown
Cauliflower	1/4	Crown
Potato	1	Medium
Salt	1/2	Teaspoon
Extra Virgin Olive Oil	1	Teaspoon

PREPARATION

1. In a blender, blend two parts peas to one part water. Continue adding water until consistency is thick but watery.

2. In a pot, bring water to a boil and add the pea broth base, and one teaspoon of extra virgin olive oil and half a teaspoon of salt. Simmer on medium-low heat for 5 minutes.

3. Dice potato into small cubes and separate the broccoli and cauliflower heads into small pieces.

4. Add the potatoes cook for 15 minutes.

5. Add the chopped celery and cook for 5 minutes.

Pea Broth Soup

6. Add the broccoli and cauliflower and cook for 5 minutes.

7. Serve & enjoy!

Entrées

Rice

Essential to any meal, making sure to cook your rice properly and perfectly is key to creating a delicious entrée. The recipes in *The Fusion Cookbook* use primarily jasmine rice and basmati rice, and less frequently, plain white rice. The recipe for these three grain types is very similar. In recipes that include rice, a brief overview of how to cook the rice is included, however be sure to refer back to this page for the full recipe whenever you are making rice!

Recipe Serves	Cook Time
2	20 Minutes

Ingredients	Amount	
Jasmine or Basmati Rice	1	Cup
Water	1 1/4	Cup
Salt	1/2	Teaspoon
Corn Oil (optional)	1	Teaspoon
Rice Vinegar (optional, for jasmine rice)	2	Tablespoons
Butter, melted (optional, for basmati rice)	1	Teaspoon

Preparation

1. Rinse your rice with water in a strainer.

2. Place the rice in a cooking pot.

3. To enhance the flavor and texture of the rice, add an optional teaspoon of corn oil and mix the rice thoroughly. For basmati rice, if you choose to use butter instead, skip this step and refer to step 9.

4. Add salt to the rice along with the oil and mix thoroughly.

5. Add water to the pot. The water should cover the rice by about half an inch.

6. Bring to a boil on high heat, then reduce heat to lowest setting.

7. Place lid on the pot and simmer for 20 minutes.

8. **For jasmine rice:** scoop rice out of pot and into a bowl. Season with optional rice vinegar and gently mix rice by folding it over itself multiple times.

RICE

9. **For basmati rice:** 5 minutes before rice is finished cooking, remove lid and add an optional teaspoon of butter, placing it on top of the rice. Replace lid and allow butter to melt, then mix thoroughly when butter is fully melted.

10. Pro tip: when the rice is finished cooking, remove the pot from the heat, keep the lid on, and let sit for approximately 10 minutes. Doing this will make the rice easier to remove and will minimize the the amount of rice that sticks to the bottom of the pot.

55

Spicy Cheesy Penne Pasta

Very cheesy, and very spicy. That's the gist of this pasta innovation! Parmesan, chili, cream and pasta – what's not to love? Take note – the flavor of this pasta entrée is striking! This pasta is best served hot and immediately upon cooking.

Recipe Serves	Cook Time
4	45 Minutes

Ingredients	Amount	
Penne Pasta	1/2	Box
Parmesan Cheese	3	Ounces
Light Cream	1/4	Cup
Chili Flakes	3/4	Teaspoon
Garlic, Crushed	1	Clove
Tomato Sauce	1	Can
Salt	1/2	Teaspoon
Black Pepper	1/2	Teaspoon
Grapeseed Oil	1	Tablespoon

PREPARATION

1. In a pot, boil water. When the water is boiled, add the penne pasta. Al Dente pasta usually takes 7 minutes, you may cook for longer depending on how firm or soft you prefer your pasta. For this recipe, it is recommended to boil the penne for 12-15 minutes on medium heat, as a softer texture goes well with this recipe.

2. Crush the clove of garlic and grate the parmesan cheese.

3. In another pot, heat the grapeseed oil under medium heat. Corn oil is a suitable alternative. When the oil is sufficiently hot, add the chili flakes and sauté for a minute or two, making sure to constantly stir to prevent burning. Caution: chili flakes will cook fast, and you don't want them to burn!

4. When the chili flakes are finished sautéing, empty into the pot the contents of one can of tomato sauce (not tomato paste!) and fill the can with water and pour that in the pot as well, so you have equal parts tomato sauce and water. Season with salt and black pepper and add the crushed

SPICY CHEESY PENNE PASTA

garlic. Stir well, bring to a boil then simmer on medium-low heat and cover the pot with a lid. Stir occasionally.

5. After 20 minutes, add a quarter cup of light cream to the pasta. Boil, then simmer for 5 minutes.

6. Add the grated parmesan cheese, boil, then simmer on low heat for 10 minutes, stirring frequently.

7. Strain the pasta, and place into a bowl, then pour the sauce over the pasta. Mix well, and serve hot!

Sesame & Chili Steak Stir Fry

A firestorm of spice, this hot chili red meat stir fry is sure to ignite all your engines. With flavors from Chinese, Vietnamese and Korean cuisines, this stir fry is bursting with a variety of flavor.

Recipe Serves	Cook Time
4	20 Minutes

Ingredients	Amount	
Steak, sliced thin	1/2	Pound
Broccoli	1/2	Crown
Red Bell Pepper	1/2	Large
Red Chili Peppers	3	Small
Baby Corn	10	Corns
Garlic, Crushed	1	Clove
Sesame Seeds	2	Tablespoons
Chili Flakes	1	Teaspoon
Black Pepper	1/2	Teaspoon
Paprika	1	Teaspoon
Peanut Oil	3	Tablespoons
Salt	1/2	Teaspoon
Jasmine Rice (optional)	1	Cup
Rice Vinegar (optional)	3	Tablespoons

Preparation

1. Slice your choice of red meat into thin slices, and place in a bowl. Marinate the steak thins with 2 tablespoons of peanut oil, and the chili flakes, sesame seeds, black pepper & paprika.

2. Crush a clove of garlic and add to the steak marinade. Mix well to ensure even coverage of seasoning.

3. Wash and break apart the broccoli. Wash and cut the red bell pepper and red chili peppers. Slice the bell pepper into long strips and cut the small chili peppers into either halves or quarters. Wash the baby corn and cut in half, either vertically or horizontally, according to personal preference.

4. Heat 1 tablespoon of peanut oil in a pan and add the steak thins. Sauté over medium heat until the exterior is cooked. Continuously toss or mix the steak thins around as you sauté.

SESAME & CHILI STEAK STIR FRY

5. Add the broccoli, red bell peppers and red chili peppers, and season with salt. Continuously stir, until vegetables and steak thins are fully cooked.

6. If served with optional jasmine rice, rinse 1 cup of rice in a strainer, then place in a pot with 1 cup of water. Bring to a boil and then simmer on lowest heat setting for 20 minutes. Season rice with salt. 3 Tablespoons of rice vinegar is optional.

Steak Thins with Tomato

What makes this dish easy to make is that the steak is cut thin, and therefore it is much easier to cook than a full-sized steak. Cooked to perfection, this dish can be eaten alone – without rice or bread. With powerful and nutritious iron and lycopene, this dish will strengthen you as it satiates.

Recipe Serves	Cook Time
3	15 Minutes

Ingredients	Amount	
Steak	1	Pound
Cherry Tomatoes	10	Tomatoes
Red Bell Pepper	1/2	Large
Garlic, crushed	1	Clove
Ginger, chopped	1	Teaspoon
Black Pepper	1/2	Teaspoon
Cayenne Pepper	1/4	Teaspoon
Peanut Oil	3	Tablespoons

Preparation

1. Slice a steak of your choice into thin slices, approximately 1 centimeter thick. For this recipe, London Broil, Petite Sirloin, or Filet Mignon are recommended, but any cut of your preference will do.

2. Slice the cherry tomatoes in half.

3. Season the steak cuts with salt, chopped ginger, crushed garlic, black pepper, and cayenne pepper, and let sit for a few minutes.

4. Heat peanut oil in a pan and add the slices.

Steak thins with Tomato

5. Once both sides of the steak cuts are cooked on the outside, add tomatoes mix well.

6. Once meat is cooked to desired redness, serve & enjoy!

Chicken Curry

In spite of being an incredibly flavorful meal, chicken curry is very easy to make! This mouth-watering, spice-laden and flavor-filled meal is best served hot, and makes for a very tasty entrée!

Recipe Serves	Cook Time
3	30 Minutes

Ingredients	Amount	
Chicken Breast	2	Breasts
Potato	1	Medium
Garlic, crushed	1	Clove
Onion	1/4	Medium
Ginger, crushed	1	Tablespoon
Cumin	1	Teaspoon
Curry Powder	1	Tablespoon
Turmeric	1	Teaspoon
Cayenne	1	Teaspoon
Crushed Tomatoes	1	Can
Plain Yogurt	1	Cup
Lemon	1	Teaspoon
Corn Oil	3	Tablespoons
Salt	1 1/2	Teaspoons
Water	3	Tablespoons
Basmati Rice	1 1/2	Cups

Preparation

1. Cut the chicken breasts into medium sized pieces and dice the potato into small cubes.

2. In a large pot heat 2 tablespoons of corn oil, add 1/2 teaspoon of salt and sauté the chicken & potato on medium heat until golden brown. When the chicken is golden on the outside, remove both ingredients from pot and set aside on a plate.

3. In the same pot that you sautéed the chicken & potato, add the minced onion, and crushed garlic & ginger, and sauté.

4. Add the curry powder, cayenne pepper, cumin, turmeric, 1 teaspoon of salt, crushed tomatoes, lemon, yogurt, and water. Mix well.

5. Add the chicken breasts & potato.

Chicken Curry

6. Cover the pot with a lid and simmer for 20 minutes on medium heat, stirring occasionally.

7. While the chicken curry is cooking, in a separate pot, cook the basmati rice (recipe given on page 54).

8. Serve, and enjoy!

Red Chili Chicken

This spicy chicken breast is seasoned to perfection! Perfectly spicy and perfectly savory, this boiled & baked chicken breast is a simple, yet incredibly flavorful meal.

Recipe Serves	Cook Time
4	50 Minutes

Ingredients	Amount	
Chicken Breast	2	Breasts
Onion	1	Medium
Cumin	1	Teaspoon
Paprika	1	Tablespoons
Chili Flakes	1 1/2	Teaspoons
Extra Virgin Olive Oil	1/4	Cup
Salt	1	Teaspoon
Sesame Seeds (optional)	1	Teaspoon

Preparation

1. Cut the chicken breasts in half, vertically.

2. Boil the chicken breasts in water for 30 minutes on medium heat, stirring occasionally.

3. Preheat the oven to 350°F.

4. While the chicken is boiling, dice the onion into very fine pieces, and mix together with salt, cumin, paprika, chili flakes and extra virgin olive oil. Set aside in a bowl.

5. When the chicken is finished boiling, take the breasts out of the pot and place in an oven safe Pyrex. Pour the chicken broth over the seasoning mix and mix well.

6. Pour the seasoned chicken broth slowly over the chicken.

Red Chili Chicken

7. Cover the Pyrex with aluminum foil and place in the oven. Bake for 20 minutes at 350°F.

8. Optional: After baking and placing on a serving plate, spread a teaspoon of sesame seeds on top of the chicken.

Chicken Parmesan in the Air Fryer

Classic Chicken Parm, only cleaner and lighter! Usually fried or deep-fried, this chicken parmesan recipe calls in the air fryer for duty, making this a much lighter and healthier option than the old way of doing things. Goes very well with chickpea soup!

Recipe Serves	Cook Time
3	16 Minutes

Ingredients	Amount	
Chicken Breast, Thin Strip	3	Strips
Parmesan Cheese	1	Ounce
Egg	1	Large
Bread Crumbs	1/2	Cup
Paprika	1	Tablespoon
Sage	1	Tablespoon
Salt	1/2	Teaspoon

Preparation

1. Crack one egg in a bowl, and whisk.

2. On a large plate, pour the breadcrumbs, and mix with paprika, sage and salt.

3. After removing any excess fat from the thin sliced chicken strips, dip each strip in the egg, covering all sides, and then dip in the bread crumb seasoning, ensuring total coverage. Repeat this with each chicken strip.

4. Preheat the air fryer at 400°F for one minute.

5. Depending on the size of your air fryer, place some or all of the chicken strips inside the air fryer and set the timer for 16 minutes. Note that the thicker your strips are, the more time will be needed to ensure that the chicken is fully cooked and safe to eat.

6. While the chicken strips are cooking, grate the parmesan cheese.

7. At 8 minutes, flip the chicken strips and place back in the air fryer to continue cooking.

8. When there are approximately 2 minutes left, remove the air fryer tray, and sprinkle the parmesan cheese on each chicken strip, and place back inside to finish cooking.

CHICKEN PARMESAN IN THE AIR FRYER

Alternative: instead of parmesan cheese, you can use chickpea soup (page 30) instead!

BREADED CHICKEN & RICE

Crispy breaded chicken served on rice with corn, peas and lima beans! Great for kids and adults alike!

Recipe Serves	Cook Time
2	20 Minutes

Ingredients	Amount	
Chicken, thin sliced	3	Slices
Bread Crumbs	1/2	Cup
Egg	1	Medium
Jasmine Rice	1/2	Cup
Cherry Tomatoes	5	Tomatoes
Salt	1/2	Teaspoon
Corn	1/4	Cup
Peas	1/4	Cup
Lima Beans	1/4	Cup
Rice Vinegar (optional)	1	Tablespoon
Jalapeño (optional)	1/4	Medium

Preparation

1. Crack one egg in a bowl, and whisk.

2. On a large plate, pour the breadcrumbs.

3. After removing any excess fat from the thin sliced chicken strips, dip each strip in the egg, covering all sides, and then dip in the bread crumb seasoning, ensuring total coverage. Repeat this with each chicken strip.

4. Preheat the air fryer at 400°F for one minute.

5. Depending on the size of your air fryer, place some or all of the chicken strips inside the air fryer and set the timer for 16 minutes. Note that the thicker your strips are, the more time will be needed to ensure that the chicken is fully cooked and safe to eat. Flip the chicken strips at 8 minutes.

6. Rinse the rice in a strainer and place in a pot, cover with water at rice level and bring to a boil. Reduce heat to lowest setting and let simmer with the lid on for 20 minutes.

7. Wash the cherry tomatoes and slice in half. Leave on the side for now.

8. In a small pot, boil water and add the frozen peas, corn and lima beans.

BREADED CHICKEN & RICE

Cook for 5 minutes, then strain and set aside.

9. When the rice is finished, place in a serving bowl and mix with the tomatoes and vegetables.

10. When the chicken is finished, slice into bite size pieces and add to the rice and vegetables. Mix well.

11. If adding the optional rice vinegar, add the tablespoon to the rice and mix well. If adding the optional jalapeño, chop a quarter of a jalapeño into small pieces and add to the rice, and mix well, then serve & enjoy!

Ginger & Basil Steak

Perfectly seasoned and deliciously juicy, these steak pieces are a great main course served alone or with rice, or as a side dish! This steak dish blends Thai and European flavors.

Recipe Serves	Cook Time
2	15 Minutes

Ingredients	Amount	
Steak	1/2	Pound
Ginger	3	Tablespoons
Basil	1	Teaspoon
Black Pepper	1/4	Teaspoon
Salt	1/2	Teaspoon
Peanut Oil	2	Tablespoons
Tomato (optional)	1/2	Medium
Jasmine Rice (optional)	1/2	Cup

Preparation

1. Slice your choice of steak into pieces, about half an inch thick.

2. Peel and crush the ginger.

3. Marinate the steak pieces in 1 tablespoon of peanut oil, basil, crushed ginger, black pepper, and salt.

4. Slice the optional tomato into thin strips. Set aside.

5. Heat 1 tablespoon of peanut oil in a pan. When hot, place the marinated steak pieces flat on the pan and cook on medium heat. Cook for 2-5 minutes, depending on how you prefer your steak (rare, medium, well done).

6. Flip steak pieces and cook for an additional 2 minutes. Add the optional tomato strips.

GINGER & BASIL STEAK

7. Serve alone or with jasmine rice (see page 54 for full rice recipe).

Breaded Chicken & Avocado

Similar to chicken parmesan, this recipe replaces parmesan with guacamole, using the popular avocado as the spread overtop the chicken. Another air fryer recipe, this recipe makes the chicken cleaner, lighter, and healthier than the fried or deep-fried variety!

Recipe Serves	Cook Time	
4	20 Minutes	

Ingredients	Amount	
Chicken Breast, Thin Strip	4	Strips
Egg	1	Large
Bread Crumbs	1/2	Cup
Avocado	1	Large
Lemon	1/2	Medium
Salt	1/2	Teaspoon

Preparation

1. Crack one egg in a bowl, and whisk. On a large plate, pour the breadcrumbs.

2. After removing any excess fat from the thin sliced chicken strips, dip each strip in the egg, covering all sides, and then dip in the breadcrumbs, ensuring total coverage. Repeat this with each chicken strip.

3. Preheat the air fryer at 400°F for one minute.

4. Depending on the size of your air fryer, place some or all of the chicken strips inside the air fryer and set the timer for 16 minutes. Note that the thicker your strips are, the more time will be needed to ensure that the chicken is fully cooked and safe to eat.

5. At 8 minutes, flip the chicken strips and place back in the air fryer to continue cooking.

6. While the chicken is cooking, cut open an avocado and remove the skin and seed. Scoop the avocado into a bowl and mash until smooth.

7. Mix lemon juice and salt in the guacamole.

Breaded Chicken & Avocado

Fusion Sushi

Sushi is normally made with sushi rice, but this recipe calls for jasmine rice. An original recipe, *The Fusion Cookbook* can't recommend it enough! Jasmine rice offers a totally unique flavor to an already delicious cuisine. Moreover, this recipe adds a little extra by including jalapeño, making the sushi not only scented with jasmine rice, but given an extra kick with hot pepper!

Recipe Serves	Cook Time
5	3 Hours

Ingredients	Amount	
Jasmine Rice	3	Cups
Seaweed	5	Sheets
Wasabi	3	Tablespoons
Sushi-Grade Tuna and Salmon	1	Pound
Baby Cucumbers	2	Medium
Red Bell Peppers	1	Large
Jalapeño	1	Medium
Pickled Ginger	3	Tablespoons
Rice Vinegar	6	Tablespoons
Sugar	1	Tablespoon
Salt	1	Teaspoons
Salmon Roe (optional)	5	Tablespoons
Uni (Sea Urchin) (optional)	5	Pieces
Bamboo or Plastic Sushi Roller (optional)		

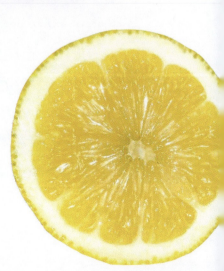

Preparation

1. Rinse the jasmine rice in a strainer, then place in cooking pot and cover with water. Pour enough water that the water exceeds the rice level by about 1-2 centimeters.

2. Bring rice to a boil, then place cover on pot, reduce heat to lowest setting, and simmer for 25 minutes.

3. When the rice is finished, remove from the pot and place in a large bowl. Add the salt, sugar and rice vinegar and mix very gently by folding the rice over itself until everything is thoroughly mixed. Cover the rice bowl with a plate and allow to sit for an hour or two, depending on the room's temperature.

4. At this point, you don't need to prepare any of the other ingredients, as the rice will need to cool down to room temperature before moving forward with the recipe. Note: when the rice is finished cooking, do NOT place in the refrigerator to accelerate the cooling process. This will damage the rice texture and will be unsuitable for an enjoyable meal. Allow the rice to cool naturally, and when the rice has reached room temperature, move on to step 5.

5. Wash the vegetables. Slice the jalapeño, baby cucumbers and red bell pepper into thin strips, lengthwise.

6. **For nigiri:** Slice your sushi-grade fish (only use sushi-grade fish for this recipe!) against the grain. When you place your rectangular block of salmon and/or tuna, you will notice lines naturally extending along the fish. Cut so that your knife is perpendicular to these lines. Slice the fish at a 45° angle and start cutting from a corner of the fish block. This will allow for longer pieces of fish to be sliced.

7. **For rolls:** slice thin strips lengthwise.

8. **For nigiri:** wet your hands with water and scoop a small amount of rice and form an elliptical shape using your palm and fingers. Place on a flat surface and gently press down, to flatten the bottom. Place your sliced fish overtop. Many sushi chefs place the wasabi underneath the fish, between the fish and the rice.

9. **For rolls:** Place your seaweed, rough side up, on a sushi roller (or on a flat surface, if you don't have one), and spread an even layer of rice over two-thirds of the seaweed, leaving the upper portion empty. Place your fish strip, and the vegetables of your choice, in the middle, extending from left to right. Roll in a forward direction, and gently press down to ensure the seaweed sticks to itself.

10. Cut individual rolls with a knife.

11. Optionally, you may place salmon roe and Uni (sea urchin) on top of the rolls for extra flavor.

Fusion Sushi

BISON PATTIES

These bison hamburger patties are unlike anything you've had before! As with all the recipes in this cookbook, this recipe is an original, and always places health as the priority! This hamburger patty recipe is an Asian-Mediterranean fusion, and provides an incredibly zesty flavor. This recipe calls for ground bison meat, though if your grocery stores doesn't carry that meat, you can certainly substitute regular ground beef.

Recipe Serves	Cook Time
4	15 Minutes

Ingredients	Amount	
Ground Bison Meat (Substitute Beef if Bison Unavailable)	1	Pound
White Onion	1/4	Onion
Red Bell Pepper	1/2	Large
Garlic, crushed	1	Clove
Ginger, crushed	1	Teaspoon
Jalapeño	1/2	Medium
Sesame Seeds	1	Teaspoon
Salt	1/2	Teaspoon
Black Pepper	1/2	Teaspoon
Cumin	1/2	Teaspoon
Paprika	1/2	Teaspoon
Sage	1/3	Teaspoon
Cayenne Pepper	1/4	Teaspoon
Peanut Oil	3	Tablespoons

Preparation

1. Crush the clove of garlic and the ginger and mix together.

2. Chop the white onion as fine as possible.

3. Chop the onion, red bell pepper, and jalapeño, all as finely as possible, and mix together.

4. Add the sesame seeds to the vegetable mix, and then add the crushed ginger & garlic, and mix everything together.

5. Add mixture to the pound of ground meat, and thoroughly mix together, ensuring an even spread throughout.

6. Divide meat into as many patties as you would like to cook. 1 pound equates to 4 hamburger sized patties.

Bison Patties

7. Heat the peanut oil in a pan and once heated, add the hamburger patties. Once cooked on one side, flip and ensure that both sides are cooked thoroughly.

8. Cooking time will depend on how you prefer your meat (rare, medium, well done, etc.). Using a utensil, you can check the redness of the interior of the patty. Note that undercooked meat can cause food poisoning.

Cinnamon Rice & Chicken

One of the simplest rice dishes, and yet absolutely bursting with flavor, cinnamon is the obvious key ingredient in this recipe. No, the rice will not come out sweet, but it will have as striking, sharp flavor that invigorates the senses.

Recipe Serves	Cook Time
10	45 Minutes

Ingredients	Amount	
Chicken Breast	1	Breast
Long Grain Parboiled Rice	1 1/2	Cups
Cinnamon	3	Tablespoons
Salt	1	Teaspoon
Corn Oil	1	Tablespoons

Preparation

1. Rinse the rice in a strainer, and then soak in water for 20 minutes.

2. Slice chicken breast into medium sized pieces

3. Sauté the chicken in oil until cooked on the outside, then cover with water (approximately 1 inch above chicken) and bring to a boil. Simmer on low heat for 20 minutes (longer if your chicken pieces are large).

4. Drain the soaked rice and in a bowl, mix rice with cinnamon and salt. Mix well to ensure even coverage.

5. Add seasoned rice to chicken pot and stir well. Cover rice with water, not higher than rice level. Bring to a boil, then simmer on low heat for 20 minutes.

6. Remove from pot, mix well and serve!

Cinnamon Rice & Chicken

Thai Stir Fry

Stir fry is a classic, though this recipe isn't! combining flavors from Thailand and the Mediterranean, this stir fry couples ginger and peanut flavors with sesame seeds and jalapeño, making an exceptionally delicious stir fry. Served with jasmine rice, this dish will fill your palate with exceptional flavors.

Recipe Serves	Cook Time
4	20 Minutes

Ingredients	Amount	
Chicken Breast	1	Breast
Garlic, crushed	1	Clove
Ginger, sliced	1	Tablespoon
Red Bell Pepper	1/2	Pepper
Green Bell Pepper	1/2	Pepper
Broccoli	1	Crown
Celery	3	Stalks
Jalapeño	1/2	Medium
Sesame Seeds	1	Teaspoon
Salt	1/2	Teaspoon
Basil	1	Teaspoon
Cayenne Pepper	1/4	Teaspoon
Chili Flakes	1/2	Teaspoon
Peanut Oil	2	Tablespoons
Jasmine Rice	1	Cup
Rice Vinegar (optional)	3	Tablespoons

PREPARATION

1. Rinse jasmine rice in a strainer, and place in a pot covered with water. Bring to a boil then simmer on lowest heat setting for 20 minutes.

2. When rice is finished, place in a bowl and mix with rice vinegar (optional) and salt.

3. Crush garlic, slice ginger into small strips, and cut bell peppers into strips. Separate broccoli into natural pieces & wash, and chop celery.

4. Cut chicken breast into thin slices, not more than half a centimeter thick. Season in a bowl with 1/2 tablespoon of peanut oil, paprika, cayenne pepper, crushed garlic, chopped basil leaves (dried or fresh), and salt.

5. Heat 1 1/2 tablespoon peanut oil in a pan and sauté chicken until cooked on the outside.

THAI STIR FRY

6. Add broccoli and celery and stir continuously.

7. When chicken is fully cooked, add bell peppers, chili flakes, and jalapeño and stir continuously until bell peppers are soft.

8. Serve with jasmine rice.

INDIAN STIR FRY

Starkly different than the other stir fry recipe featured in *The Fusion Cookbook*, this stir fry combines Thai and Indian flavors. Combining ginger & basil with turmeric, this unique rice dish will be sure to surprise the palate.

Recipe Serves	Cook Time	
4	20 Minutes	
Ingredients	**Amount**	
Chicken Breast	1	Breast
Garlic, crushed	1	Clove
Red Bell Pepper	1/2	Pepper
Green Bell Pepper	1/2	Pepper
Cauliflower	1	Crown
Broccoli	1	Crown
Jalapeño	1/2	Medium
Turmeric	2	Teaspoons
Sage	1	Teaspoon
Basil, chopped	1	Tablespoon
Chili Flakes	1/2	Teaspoon
Salt	1/2	Teaspoon
Walnut Oil	2	Tablespoons
Basmati Rice	1	Cup

Preparation

1. Rinse basmati rice in a strainer, and place in a pot covered with water. Bring to a boil then simmer on lowest heat setting for 20 minutes.

2. When rice is finished, place in a bowl and season with salt.

3. Crush garlic and cut bell peppers into strips. Separate cauliflower and broccoli into natural pieces & wash, and chop celery.

4. Cut chicken breast into thin slices, not more than half a centimeter thick. Season in a bowl with 1/2 tablespoon of walnut oil, turmeric, sage, crushed garlic, chopped basil, and salt.

5. Heat 1 1/2 tablespoon walnut oil in a pan and sauté chicken until cooked on the outside.

Indian Stir Fry

6. Add broccoli, cauliflower & celery and stir continuously, adding a dash of turmeric powder.

7. When chicken is fully cooked, add bell peppers, chili flakes, and jalapeño and stir continuously until bell peppers are soft.

8. Serve with basmati rice.

GARLIC & GINGER SPAGHETTI

One of the more innovative recipes in *The Fusion Cookbook*, this spaghetti is anything but classic. Mixing East Asian with Italian, this recipe calls for ginger as a core flavor to the meat sauce.

Recipe Serves	Cook Time
6	40 Minutes

Ingredients	Amount	
Whole Wheat Spaghetti	3/4	Pound
Ground Meat (Bison or Beef)	1/2	Pound
Tomato Sauce	1	Can
Garlic	1	Clove
Ginger, crushed	1	Heaping Tablespoon
Broccoli	1/2	Crown
Corn	1/2	Cup
Sesame Seeds	1	Tablespoon
Black Pepper	1/2	Teaspoon
Sage	1/2	Teaspoon
Basil	1/2	Teaspoon
Salt	1/2	Teaspoon
Walnut Oil	1	Tablespoon

PREPARATION

1. Place the raw ground meat in a bowl, and season with a crushed garlic clove, crushed ginger, sesame seeds, black pepper, sage, basil, and salt. Mix thoroughly.

2. In a pot, heat the walnut oil and sauté the ground meat until cooked on the outside. This recipe recommends bison, though beef is a perfectly fine substitute.

3. In another pot, empty the contents of one can of tomato sauce, and equal parts water. Season with a dash of salt and black pepper. Bring to a boil then reduce heat to medium and allow to simmer.

4. When the meat is sufficiently cooked on the outside, though still not fully cooked on the inside, pour into the pot of simmering tomato sauce. Bring to a boil then simmer on medium heat, covered, for 20 minutes, stirring frequently.

5. In a separate pot, bring water, salt and a few drops of cooking oil to a boil and add the spaghetti. Al Dente is achieved after 6-7 minutes of boiling, though you may desire to boil for longer depending on personal preference. When the spaghetti is finished, strain and set aside in a large bowl.

6. In another pot, bring water and a dash of salt to a boil and add the corn. After boiling for 5 minutes, add the broccoli, which has been broken apart into medium and small pieces. Boil the broccoli for 4-5 minutes, depending on firmness preference. Strain and place over the spaghetti.

7. When the meat sauce is finished, pour directly over the spaghetti and vegetables, and mix thoroughly.

8. Add additional salt and black pepper to preference, and enjoy!

GARLIC & GINGER SPAGHETTI

LEMON & ROSEMARY CHICKEN

A zesty chicken and rice dish that is as unique as it is flavorful! Lemon, garlic and rosemary form the seasoning, and this dish can be served as a stew, rice dish, or even a hearty soup!

Recipe Serves	Preparation Time
4	40 Minutes

Ingredients	Amount	
Chicken Breast	2	Breasts
Russet Potatoes	3	Medium
Garlic	2	Cloves
Lemon	1	Large
Extra Virgin Olive Oil	3	Tablespoons
Rosemary	1/4	Teaspoon
Salt	1	Teaspoon
Basmati Rice	1 1/2	Cups
Cilantro (optional)	1/4	Bunch

Preparation

1. Cut the skinless, boneless chicken breast into medium sized chunks.

2. Crush the garlic cloves.

3. Squeeze the lemon.

4. Peel and dice the potatoes into medium sized chunks, about the same size as the chicken.

5. Sauté the chicken and then add water and bring to a boil. The water should be about 1 inch above the chicken. Simmer on medium heat for 15 minutes.

6. Add the potatoes, garlic, lemon juice, rosemary, and salt to the pot and simmer on medium heat for 20 minutes.

7. While the chicken and potatoes are cooking, cook the basmati rice (full recipe on page 54).

8. The chicken and potatoes, when finished cooking, should be sitting in water that is level with the food. This dish is primarily a rice dish, but can be served as a soup.

9. Add a handful of optional cilantro leaves when serving.

10. Serve with basmati rice and enjoy!

Lemon & Rosemary Chicken

Meat 'n Wheat Patties

This dish comes from the Mediterranean region, and mixes red meat with cracked wheat, to produce a delicious, fiber- and protein-packed lunch or dinner that keeps you full for longer! This patty is minimally seasoned and has a wonderfully unique texture!

Recipe Serves	Preparation Time	
2	30 Minutes	
Ingredients	**Amount**	
Red Meat	1	Pound
Cracked Wheat (Bulgur Wheat)	1/2	Cup
White Onion	1/4	Small
Salt	1/2	Teaspoon
Cumin	1/2	Teaspoon
Salt	1	Teaspoon
Black Pepper	1/4	Teaspoon
Jalapeño (optional)	1/4	Medium

Preparation

1. Rise and soak the cracked wheat in a bowl of water for 15-20 minutes. You may need to add water throughout as the wheat will absorb some water. Soaking in water will soften the wheat. If you skip this step, the texture of the final product will be grainy.

2. Chop the steak into medium sized pieces, and place in a food processor. Likewise chop a quarter of a small white onion, jalapeño, and place in the food processor.

3. Strain the water from the cracked wheat and add to the food processor, and blend together for a minute or two.

4. Scoop the mixture into a bowl or plate, and then form thin patties with your hands.

5. You may place the patties in an air fryer and cook at 400°F for 16 minutes, flipping at 8 minutes, or you may pan fry with a little cooking oil, flipping until cooked on both sides and internally.

6. You may also cook on a pan. Place a small amount of cooking oil and heat on medium heat, then cook each patty individually, flipping so it is cooked on both sides.

Meat 'n Wheat Patties

Beef & Broccoli

A healthier take on a beloved classic, this beef & broccoli is seasoned with ginger and sesame seeds – and without soy sauce, making it a lower sodium version of this classic dish. A fusion dish, this dish doesn't use jasmine or sticky rice, but rather plain, American white rice. Optionally spicy, this beef & broccoli is best served hot!

Recipe Serves	Preparation Time
2	30 Minutes

Ingredients	Amount	
Long Grain White Rice	1	Cup
Steak (Beef)	1	Pound
Ginger	1/4	Cup
Broccoli	1	Large Crown
Sesame Seeds	1	Teaspoon
White Onion	1/4	Small
Salt	1	Teaspoon
Black Pepper	1/4	Teaspoon
Corn Oil	1	Tablespoon
Jalapeño (optional)	1/4	Medium

Preparation

1. Prepare the rice and set aside (full recipe on page 54).

2. Heat water in a pot and bring to a boil.

3. While the water is heating to a boil, cut the steak into small strips, and set aside.

4. Break apart the broccoli florets into natural pieces, and rinse in a strainer.

5. Take one quarter of a small white onion, and slice into thin strips, and set aside.

6. Peel the ginger, and slice into strips, about half the size as the strips of meat.

7. When the water reaches a boil, add the broccoli and cook for 2 minutes, then take out and place in a strainer, allowing the broccoli to dry as much as possible.

8. Pour the corn oil in a frying pan and pre-heat on medium heat.

BEEF & BROCCOLI

9. When the oil is hot, add the onion and season with black pepper, and sauté.

10. Add the steak strips, ginger salt, and optional jalapeño, and cook on medium heat until medium-well, or per your preference.

11. When the steak is nearly finished, add the sesame seeds and broccoli to the pan and mix well. Cook for an additional minute, then serve over white rice, and enjoy!

Mediterranean Taco Salad

A fusion recipe combining Mexican and Mediterranean flavors, this taco salad can be served as a main course or as a salad. Replacing cheddar cheese with Bulgarian feta, and adding flavors like cilantro this taco salad beautifully combines the flavors of Mexico and the Mediterranean!

Recipe Serves	Preparation Time
2	30 Minutes

Ingredients	Amount	
Ground Meat	1	Pound
Bulgarian Feta Cheese	1/4	Pound
Red Bell Pepper	1/4	Medium
Green Bell Pepper	1/4	Medium
Persian Cucumbers	2	Medium
Tomato	1	Medium
White Onion	1	Tablespoon
Jalapeno	1/4	Medium
Romaine Lettuce	4	Leaves
Cilantro	1/4	Bunch
Salt	1/2	Teaspoon
Black Pepper	1/2	Teaspoon
Cumin	1/4	Teaspoon
Paprika	1/2	Teaspoon
Cayenne Pepper	1/2	Teaspoon
Water	2	Tablespoons
Tortilla Chips	1/2	Bag
Cheddar Cheese, grated (optional)	1/4	Cup

PREPARATION

1. Place the ground meat in a cooking pot and add the salt, black pepper, cumin, paprika, and cayenne pepper and mix well, ensuring the seasoning is equally distributed.

2. Add two tablespoons of water to the meat and cook on medium heat for 10 minutes, stirring frequently. When finished, set aside.

3. Chop the tomato, cucumber, red & green bell peppers, onion, jalapeño, cilantro, and romaine lettuce, and place each ingredient in separate bowls.

4. Break apart the feta cheese. Feta cheese naturally crumbles when broken apart. Place in a bowl.

5. Alternatively, if you prefer a classic taco salad, use freshly grated cheddar cheese instead of feta cheese. If you use cheddar, do not include cilantro in this recipe.

6. Put your desired amount of meat in a bowl or plate, and then begin adding the other ingredients, according to your desired ratio.

7. Mix everything together in your individual serving plate, and enjoy with tortilla chips! The tortilla chips may be broken into smaller pieces and added to the salad mix, or used full size as scooping chips.

MEDITERRANEAN TACO SALAD

GINGER STEAK WITH RICE

Combining Asian, Persian and American flavors, this fusion dish incorporates ginger and Basmati rice with steak, tomato and onion, creating an aromatic entrée that will delight the senses!

Recipe Serves	Preparation Time
2	30 Minutes

Ingredients	Amount	
Beef	1/2	Pound
Ginger, sliced	2	Tablespoons
Cherry Tomatoes	5	Tomatoes
Onion	1/4	Medium
Salt	1/2	Teaspoon
Black Pepper	1/4	Teaspoon
Basmati Rice	1/2	Cup
Corn Oil	1	Tablespoon

Preparation

1. Cook the Basmati rice (full recipe on page 54).

2. Slice the steak into thin strips.

3. Peel & slice the ginger into thin strips.

4. Cut the onion lengthwise into strips.

5. Wash & cut the cherry tomatoes into halves, lengthwise.

6. Heat the corn oil in a pan on medium heat and then add the onion, and sauté with the salt and black pepper, until golden brown.

7. Add the steak strips to the pan, mixing & flipping frequently, cooking on medium heat.

8. After 3 minutes of cooking, add the ginger strips, continuing to stir & mix frequently, and continue cooking for another 3 minutes, then add the cherry tomatoes, continuing to mix frequently.

9. Continue cooking until the meat has cooked to medium, or your desired preference.

10. Serve with basmati rice, and enjoy!

Ginger Steak With Rice

Red Meat Marinade

While not an actual entrée, this marinade serves as the base for a red meat entrée of your choice. This marinade can be used as an overnight marinade, or as a quick flavor enhancer before cooking. In either case, the sharp flavor will upgrade any red meat recipe!

Recipe Serves	Preparation Time
N/A	10 Minutes

Ingredients	Amount	
Basil	10	Leaves
Mint	10	Leaves
Garlic	2	Cloves
Parsley	1/4	Bunch
Extra Virgin Olive Oil	3	Tablespoons
Lemon Zest	1	Teaspoon
Lemon Juice	1/2	Medium Lemon
Thyme	1	Teaspoon
Black Pepper	1/2	Teaspoon
Cayenne Pepper	1/2	Teaspoon
Salt	1/2	Teaspoon

Preparation

1. Wash the separate the mint and basil leaves from their stems.

2. Grate the lemon skin and squeeze half the lemon.

3. Crush the garlic cloves.

4. Chop the parsley, using only the leaves, not the stems.

5. Place all ingredients in the food processor and add the thyme and other seasonings.

6. Blend in the food processor until consistency is paste.

7. Add more ingredients in equal proportion relative to how much red meat you intend to marinate.

RED MEAT MARINADE

Vinegar & Mustard Marinade

Another marinade, this can be used on red meat and chicken alike. This marinade offers an all-American flavor, and can be used on meat that is BBQ'd, pan-seared or meat used in stir fry!

Recipe Serves	Preparation Time	
N/A	10 Minutes	
Ingredients	**Amount**	
Balsamic Vinegar	3	Tablespoons
Spicy Brown Mustard	2	Tablespoons
Olive Oil	3	Tablespoons
Sage	1/2	Tablespoon
Paprika	1/4	Tablespoon
Salt	1	Teaspoon
Black Pepper	1/4	Teaspoon

Preparation

1. Prepare the meat of choice on a plate and drizzle the olive oil and balsamic vinegar evenly over the meat.

2. Do the same with the spicy brown mustard.

3. Using a utensil or your hand, rub the mustard and vinegar into the meat so it is spread evenly.

4. Sprinkle the sage, paprika, salt and black pepper evenly.

5. Rub the ingredients again so that everything is mixed and spread evenly across the meat.

VINEGAR & MUSTARD MARINADE

6. Flip the meat and rub the ingredients on the other side. Repeat this step a couple more times.

7. Add more ingredients in equal proportion relative to how much meat you intend to marinate.

Sides

Chili Potatoes

Caution: very spicy! These boiled potatoes will have you ignited on all cylinders. Sautéed in chili flakes and olive oil, this dish serves as an excellent side to eggs, meat, or any other starch-friendly meal!

Recipe Serves	Cook Time
4	30 Minutes

Ingredients	Amount	
Russet Potatoes	4	Large
Yellow Onion	1	Small
Chili Flakes	1 1/2	Teaspoons
Cumin	1	Teaspoons
Paprika	1	Tablespoon
Extra Virgin Olive Oil	1/4	Cup
Salt	1	Teaspoon
Bread (optional)		

Preparation

1. Dice the potatoes into medium sized chunks and place in a pot of boiling water. Cook for 15 minutes on medium heat.

2. Mince the onion into very fine pieces, and mix together with the cumin, salt, paprika, chili flakes, and olive oil.

3. Sauté the onions & seasoning in a pan on low heat, stirring continuously, then place cover over pan and simmer for 20 minutes on low heat, stirring occasionally.

4. Drain the potatoes and place in the pan with the simmering onions, mix together, and continue simmering for 10 minutes, stirring once or twice.

5. Can be eaten with alone, with bread, or as a side dish to a variety of other recipes.

Chili Potatoes

Feta Cheese & Vegetables

This recipe makes for an excellent snack, light lunch, post-meal spread, and can be eaten any time of day! A truly versatile meal, this serves as a great dessert alternative, breakfast, or lunch in and of itself!

Recipe Serves	Preparation Time
4	5 Minutes

Ingredients	Amount	
Feta Cheese	1/4	Pound
Baby Cucumbers	4	Medium
Tomato	1	Large
Parsley	1/4	Bunch
Mint Leaves (optional)	4	Stems
Radish (optional)	4	Small
Pickled Cornichons (optional)	1	Ounce
Salt	1/4	Teaspoon
Pita Bread	1	Pita

Preparation

1. Serve the feta cheese as a single block.

2. Wash and peel several baby cucumbers and a large juicy tomato. Chop the parsley very coarse and loose.

3. Slice the vegetables into bite size pieces. Pro tip: cutting your vegetables diagonally makes them appear more appetizing.

4. Mint leaves, and radishes go well with this meal, but are optional. Rinse the mint and discard the stems. Dice the radishes.

5. On a separate plate, serve several picked cornichons.

6. Heat pita bread and serve as a light snack or as an after-meal platter!

FETA CHEESE & VEGETABLES

SALSA

A classic side dish for every dinner party! Salsa is world famous for its crisp and spicy flavor, and this salsa recipe will thoroughly invigorate the senses!

Recipe Serves	Preparation Time
4	10 Minutes

Ingredients	Amount	
Tomatoes	5	Medium
Cilantro	1	Bunch
White Onion	1	Small
Jalapeño	1	Medium
Olive Oil	1	Teaspoon
Salt	1/2	Teaspoon
Cumin	1/2	Teaspoon
Black Pepper	1/4	Teaspoon
Tomato Sauce (optional)	3	Tablespoons

Preparation

1. Finely chop the white onion and tomatoes. Though not necessary, peeling 2 of the 5 tomatoes, before chopping them, will give the salsa a better texture. The onion shouldn't be too large otherwise its flavor will overpower the salsa.

2. Chop the jalapeño and add to the onion and tomatoes.

3. Wash the cilantro and remove the leaves from the stems, and coarsely chop.

4. Season the salsa with salt, cumin, olive oil, and black pepper.

SALSA

5. If you prefer your salsa to be a bit thicker you may add the optional tomato sauce. This will also enhance the color of the salsa.

RESTAURANT STYLE SALSA

While still salsa, this salsa is completely different than the one on the previous page! Smooth and restaurant style, this salsa is incredibly easy to make and great to serve at a dinner party!

Recipe Serves	Preparation Time	
4	10 Minutes	|//
Ingredients	**Amount**	
Tomatoes	5	Medium
Cilantro	1	Bunch
Garlic	1	Clove
White Onion	1/2	Medium
Jalapeño	1	Medium
Red Bell Pepper	1	Medium
Lime	1	Medium
Salt	1/2	Teaspoon
Cumin	1	Teaspoon
Black Pepper	1/4	Teaspoon

Preparation

1. Wash the tomatoes, bell pepper, jalapeño and cilantro bunch, and add to a food processor.

2. Add the garlic clove and half onion to the food processor.

3. Squeeze the lime and add the juice to the food processor, along with the salt, black pepper and cumin.

4. Blend on low or medium until silky smooth – usually 20-30 seconds depending on the power of your food processor.

5. Empty contents into a bowl, serve with salsa chips and enjoy!

Restaurant Style Salsa

Hummus

Sure, this recipe isn't a *Fusion Cookbook* original, but who doesn't love hummus as a side dish, vegetable dip, or sandwich spread? Not a fusion recipe, this recipe is the real deal Mediterranean way of doing it!

Recipe Serves	Preparation Time
6	10 Minutes

Ingredients	Amount	
Chickpeas, cooked	2	Cups
Lemon	1/2	Cup
Garlic	1	Clove
Tahini Paste	1/2	Cup
Salt	1/2	Teaspoon
Cayenne Pepper (optional)	1	Teaspoon

Preparation

1. Strain the chickpeas and rinse with running water. Though not necessary, if you want to make your hummus taste extra-gourmet, remove the clear, cellulose skin from each chickpea. This isn't as time consuming as it may sound, and it will make the texture of the finished product far superior.

HUMMUS

2. Place chickpeas in food processor and sprinkle with salt. Canned chickpeas may be added as is; dried chickpeas must be cooked first.

3. Squeeze the lemon and pour juice over chickpeas.

4. Add the tahini paste to the chickpeas.

5. Add the garlic clove to the mix.

6. Add approximately a quarter cup of water. Adding too much water will ruin the consistency, so better to add a small amount, blend the mix, and slowly add small amounts more if necessary.

7. Blend everything in the processor until thick and smooth.

8. Scoop out of the processor and onto your serving plate, and sprinkle with the optional cayenne pepper.

9. Serve with vegetables, bread or crackers, and enjoy!

Crispy Thyme Potatoes

Absolutely crispy on the outside and soft as butter on the inside, these potatoes will add an arsenal of flavor to any dinner table spread. Flavored with thyme and garlic, and textured by boiling and grilling, these potatoes are truly unique!

Recipe Serves	Cook Time
6	60 Minutes

Ingredients	Amount	
Potatoes	5	Large
Garlic	3	Cloves
Thyme	3	Tablespoons
Extra Virgin Olive Oil	5	Tablespoons
Salt	1	Teaspoon
Black Pepper	1/2	Teaspoon

Preparation

1. Preheat the oven to 350°F.

2. Prepare a pot of boiling water. Add a dash of salt and 2-3 drops of extra virgin olive oil (or corn oil) to the water.

3. While the water is heating up, crush the garlic cloves and peel & cut the potatoes into large cubes. Mix the thyme, salt and black pepper with the crushed garlic and 2 tablespoons of extra virgin olive oil.

4. Boil the large potato chunks for 10 minutes. Remove from pot and strain.

5. Place the potatoes on a large baking sheet, evenly spread apart.

6. Drizzle 3 tablespoons of extra virgin olive oil generously over the potatoes, and season with the olive oil, garlic, thyme, salt, and black pepper mixture. Make sure to evenly cover each side of the potato cubes.

Crispy Thyme Potatoes

7. Place the potatoes in the oven and bake for one hour.

8. Halfway through, remove the potatoes and turn, so as to evenly cook the cubes. Place back in the oven. Note: be sure that when you open and close the oven, be quick about it, so that you don't lose too much heat!

9. When the potatoes are finished baking, they should be crispy on the outside and soft on the inside.

Indian Style Potatoes & Vegetables

Neither spicy nor bland, these spice-covered vegetables make a great sidekick to any rice or red meat dish! Combining flavors from India, the Mediterranean and Southern Europe, these vegetables are as healthy as they are delicious!

Recipe Serves	Cook Time	
2	20 Minutes	
Ingredients	**Amount**	
Potato	1	Large
Cauliflower	1/4	Crown
Peas	1/2	Cup
Corn	1/3	Cup
Turmeric	1 1/2	Tablespoon
Sage	1	Tablespoon
Salt	1/2	Teaspoon
Grapeseed Oil	1/2	Teaspoon

Preparation

1. Dice one large russet potato into large pieces

2. Bring water to boil in a pot, add a dash of salt and grapeseed oil, and toss in the potatoes. Boil for 20 minutes.

3. In a separate pot, bring water to a boil and add a dash of grapeseed oil and salt.

4. When the water has reached a boil, add the peas, and let cook for 5 minutes.

5. Add the corn and cook for 5 minutes.

6. While the corn and peas are cooking, separate the cauliflower heads into medium sized pieces, and rub turmeric and sage onto the cauliflower heads. Don't just sprinkle the seasoning over top, but actively rub it into the vegetable, to ensure the flavor sticks to the cauliflower.

7. Add the cauliflower to the peas and corn, and boil for 5-7 minutes.

8. Strain the vegetables, and the potatoes, and mix together in a bowl. Add salt and enjoy!

INDIAN STYLE POTATOES & VEGETABLES

Brussels Sprouts in the Air Fryer

Another air fryer recipe, these Brussels sprouts are crispy on the outside, and soft on the inside. Flavored with herbs like oregano and cayenne, and marinaded in peanut oil, these Brussel sprouts carry with them hints of Thanksgiving dinner.

Recipe Serves	Cook Time
6	15 Minutes

Ingredients	Amount	
Brussel Sprouts	20	Sprouts
Black Pepper	1	Teaspoon
Cayenne Pepper	1/2	Teaspoon
Oregano	2	Teaspoons
Lemon	1/2	Medium
Salt	1/2	Teaspoon
Peanut Oil	2	Tablespoons
Coarse Salt (optional)	1	Pinch

Preparation

1. Rinse the Brussels sprouts and remove the outermost layer.

2. Slice each Brussel sprout in half, vertically.

3. Season with lemon juice, peanut oil, oregano, cayenne pepper and black pepper. Do not add the salt yet.

4. Mix to ensure even coverage and let sit for 5 minutes.

5. Season with salt and mix together.

6. Place in a preheated air fryer at 400°F for 15 minutes. At each 5-minute interval, remove the air fryer basket and toss the Brussel sprouts around to ensure even cooking.

Brussels Sprouts in the Air Fryer

7. When the Brussel sprouts are finished cooking, place on serving plate and season with coarse salt, optional.

8. Serve as a delightful side dish, and enjoy!

Dill & Lima Bean Rice

This Persian rice dish is exquisitely refreshing, with the sharp flavor of dill and the delicate texture of cooked lima beans. It is surprisingly easy to make and doesn't take much time at all!

Recipe Serves	Cook Time
6	30 Minutes

Ingredients	Amount	
Basmati Rice	2	Cups
Fresh Dill	1	Bunch
Lima Beans	1	Cup
Salt	1/2	Teaspoon
Grapeseed Oil	1	Teaspoon
Butter, melted (optional)	1	Tablespoon

Preparation

1. Rinse the basmati rice in a strainer, then place in a cooking pot and cover with 3 cups of water. Add a tablespoon of grapeseed oil and salt and mix together.

2. Bring to a boil, then reduce heat to low, cover, and simmer for 15 minutes.

3. In another pot, bring water to a boil, and cook the lima beans for 10 minutes. Once the beans are finished, strain and set aside.

4. While the rice is simmering, wash and chop the dill into fine pieces.

5. When the rice has simmered for 15 minutes, remove the cover, and add the chopped dill and mix together thoroughly. Once the dill and rice are mixed together, add the lima beans on the top and spread evenly (do not mix).

6. Put the cover back on the pot and continue simmering for another 15 minutes.

Dill & Lima Bean Rice

7. When the rice is finished, remove from pot and place in a serving bowl, and mix well. Add salt, if necessary, according to taste.

8. Optional: melt a small amount of butter, equalling approximately 1 tablespoon melted, and pour over the rice, then mix thoroughly.

Vegetable Rice

There is nothing wrong with a simple rice dish, especially when it can be as delicious as this one! Jasmine rice, steamed with celery, peas, corn and seasoned with rice vinegar, this rice dish, though simple, is incredibly complex in its flavor distribution.

Recipe Serves	Cook Time
4	20 Minutes

Ingredients	Amount	
Jasmine Rice	1	Cup
Peas	1/4	Cup
Corn	1/4	Cup
Celery	4	Stalks
Salt	1	Teaspoon
Rice Vinegar	3	Tablespoons
Broccoli (optional)	1/4	Crown

Preparation

1. Rinse jasmine rice, and place in pot covered with water. Bring to a boil then simmer on lowest heat setting for 20 minutes.

2. When rice is finished, season with salt and rice vinegar and mix well.

3. In a separate pot, bring water to a boil and add chopped celery. Cook for 5 minutes on medium heat.

4. Add peas to the boiling celery and cook for 5 minutes.

5. Add corn and cook for 5 minutes.

6. Optional: add broccoli to boiling water with the

Vegetable Rice

corn, and cook for 5 minutes.

7. Strain vegetables and add to rice. Mix well and serve.

Baked Feta Cheese

Surprise yourself with a unique and innovative sandwich! This Mediterranean-French twist will delight your palate with notes of the Mediterranean Sea coupled with scents of Parisian sandwich shops. This melted cheese works as a dip, or as sandwich filler. If you're feeling adventurous you can even use it as a heavy pasta sauce.

Recipe Serves	Cook Time
4	45 Minutes

Ingredients	Amount	
Feta Cheese	1/2	Pound
Cherry Tomatoes	6	Pieces
Salt	1/2	Teaspoon
Extra Virgin Olive Oil	2	Teaspoons
Jalapeño (optional)	1/4	Small
Bread (optional)		

Preparation

1. Preheat the oven to 350°F.

2. Crumble the feta cheese into small pieces, and place in an oven friendly Pyrex glass cooking pan.

3. Slice the cherry tomatoes in half and mix into the cheese evenly.

4. Dice the optional jalapeño and add to the cheese as well.

5. Drizzle the cheese and vegetable medley with olive oil and a dash of salt, and cover with aluminum foil.

6. Place in an oven, preheated to 350°F, for 30 minutes.

7. When ready, this melted cheese dish can be used as a dip for vegetables and crackers or can be poured onto a heated baguette for a delicious cheese sandwich.

Baked Feta Cheese

123

French Fries in the Air Fryer

While *The Fusion Cookbook* didn't invent the french fry, it definitely combines herbs from different parts of the world. Peanut oil, sage and paprika make the bulk of the seasoning, and when cooked in the air fryer, the scent, flavor and texture balance out perfectly on the palate.

Recipe Serves	Cook Time
2	25 Minutes

Ingredients	Amount	
Potatoes	3	Large
Peanut Oil	1	Tablespoon
Sage	1	Teaspoon
Paprika	1	Teaspoon
Salt	1/2	Teaspoon

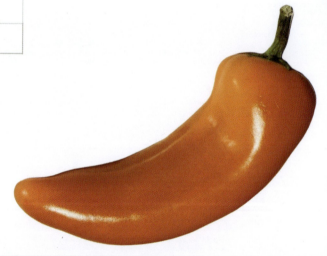

Preparation

1. Slice the potatoes into evenly sized wedges. Pro Tip: Cutting the potatoes at an angle, so that one side of the wedge is wide, and the other side is more pointed, will provide a most appetizing bite.

2. Place the cut wedges in a bowl, and drizzle the peanut oil, salt, sage and paprika, and mix very well with your hands so that every wedge is evenly coated with the oil & seasoning.

3. Place the wedges in your air fryer and air fry at 400°F for 25 minutes.

4. Every 8 minutes or so, remove the tray and shake/flip is so that the wedges get evenly cooked on all sides.

5. When finished, serve and enjoy hot, or save for later!

French Fries in the air fryer

Fusion Nachos

Combining classic nachos with Mediterranean flavor, Fusion Nachos include Lebanese green olives as the signature flavor. These nachos are deliciously appetizing and great for movie night, or simply as a side dish at the dinner table!

Recipe Serves	Cook Time
2	5 Minutes

Ingredients	Amount	
Sharp Cheddar Cheese, grated	1/2	Cup
Tomato	1/2	Medium
Olives	10	Olives
Black Pepper	1/4	Teaspoon
Tortilla Chips	1/2	Bag
Jalapeño (optional)	1/4	Medium

Preparation

1. Turn the oven on broil, low heat, and preheat the oven.

2. Spread the tortilla chips evenly on an oven safe tray or a Pyrex.

3. Slice the tomato into very thin slices and lay over the tortilla chips.

4. Grate the cheddar cheese, then cover evenly over the tomatoes & tortilla chips.

5. Chop the optional jalapeño into small pieces and spread over the cheese.

6. Season the nachos with black pepper, and place in the oven on the top rack.

7. Cook for 5 minutes or until the cheese is fully melted, then take out of the oven.

FUSION NACHOS

8. While the nachos are in the oven, remove the seeds from the green olives and then cut each olive into halves or quarters. Spread evenly over the melted nachos when they have finished cooking.

9. Serve, and enjoy!

Quinoa & Avocado

This delicious quinoa dish is chock full of fiber and nutrients, and the quinoa's texture is balanced perfectly with soft avocado! This meal is incredibly filling, and is best served chilled!

Recipe Serves	Cook Time
6	30 Minutes

Ingredients	Amount	
Quinoa	2	Cups
Red Bell Pepper	1	Medium
Avocado	1	Medium
Back Beans	1	Can
Corn	1	Cup
Tomato, diced	1	Cup
White Onion, chopped	1/4	Cup
Cilantro	1/2	Bunch
Lemon	1/2	Medium
Salt	1/2	Teaspoon
Paprika	1	Teaspoon
Cayenne Pepper	1/2	Teaspoon
Water	4	Cups

Preparation

1. Chop the red bell pepper into small pieces, and dice the tomato and white onion. Place in a cooking pot.

2. Strain and rinse the black beans in a strainer and add to the pot. Canned beans may be added as is, while dried beans must be cooked first.

3. Add the corn to the pot. Frozen corn may be used.

4. Add the quinoa and the water to the pot and mix well. Add the salt, cayenne pepper & paprika and mix well.

5. Bring to a boil on high heat, then reduce heat to medium-low and cook with the lid on for 20 minutes.

6. When finished cooking, remove from pot and place in a bowl and allow to cool at room temperature. Do not place in fridge to cool down faster, as this will ruin the texture and flavor of the dish!

Quinoa & Avocado

7. When the quinoa has reached room temperature, chop the cilantro and squeeze the half lemon, and add to the dish, and mix well.

8. Place in the fridge and allow to cool.

9. When ready to serve, slice an avocado and add to the individual serving bowls, and enjoy!

SWEETS

Banana Pumpkin Cake

Heavy and dense without using too much oil, this banana bread, flavored with pumpkin spice & vanilla extract, will definitely satiate any sweet tooth you may have! Carrying flavors of autumn and winter, this bread/cake goes well with morning coffee, or with vanilla ice cream after a delicious meal!

Recipe Serves	Cook Time
8	90 Minutes

Ingredients	Amount	
Bananas, Brown	4	Large
Eggs	2	Large
Corn Oil	3	Tablespoons
Sugar	2	Tablespoons
Flour	1 1/2	Cups
Baking Soda	1	Teaspoon
Baking Powder	1	Teaspoon
Vanilla Extract	1	Teaspoon
Pumpkin Spice Seasoning	1	Teaspoon
Salt	1/2	Teaspoon
Date Fruit, chopped	5	Pieces
Walnuts (optional)	10	Halves

Preparation

1. Preheat the oven to 350°F.

2. Crack 2 eggs in a bowl and whisk together with corn oil and sugar, in a large mixing bowl.

3. Slowly add flour and whisk well.

4. Add the baking soda, baking powder, and salt and whisk together with the previous ingredients.

5. Add the vanilla extract and pumpkin spice and mix well.

6. In a separate bowl, mash the bananas. This recipe requires that the bananas be spotted brown. In other words, make sure they are a few days old. They should be soft and sweet.

7. Add the bananas to the mix and whisk very well, ensuring that everything has been completely mixed.

8. Remove the seeds from the dates, and chop each date into 4-5 pieces, then add to the batter and mix well.

9. Sprinkle flour in your baking pan, making sure to lightly cover the bottom and sides. Pour the batter into the pan, place the optional walnut halves on top of the batter, and place in the oven.

10. Depending on the ripeness of the bananas, the cooking time for this recipe varies. At the 45-minute mark, remove the bread from there oven and stick a butter knife down the center of the bread. If it comes out perfectly clean, the bread is ready. If not, place the bread back in the oven for another 20 minutes.

11. Continue this process until the bread is ready, ensuring that you allow as little heat as possible from escaping the oven each time you open & close the oven door.

Banana Pumpkin Cake

Very Fluffy Pancakes

These pancakes are silky smooth, fluffy and absolutely fruity! Perfect for a cozy morning during a snowstorm, or late evening for a midnight snack, these pancakes are best served hot!

Recipe Serves	Cook Time
6	15 Minutes

Ingredients	Amount	
Flour	1 1/2	Cups
Eggs	1	Large
Milk	1 1/4	Cups
Baking Powder	2 1/2	Teaspoons
Salt	1/4	Teaspoon
Vanilla Extract	1	Tablespoon
Corn Oil	3	Tablespoons
Crushed Blueberry (optional)	3	Tablespoons
Banana Slices (optional)	1	Banana
Jam (optional)	3	Tablespoons

Preparation

1. Crack 1 egg in a bowl and whisk.

2. Add 2 tablespoons of corn oil, flour, baking powder, salt and milk to the whisked egg, and whisk together until mixture is silky smooth.

3. If choosing to add optional blueberry, rinse blueberries in a strainer, and then crush in a cup or bowl and add to pancake mixture.

4. Pour 1 tablespoon of corn oil on a pan and heat on high heat.

5. When oil is hot, reduce heat to medium and pour part of the pancake mixture on the pan, size according to personal preference.

6. When pancake is cooked on the bottom, flip to ensure both sides are cooked. When pancake is fully cooked, remove from heat and place on serving plate.

7. Serve with optional banana and jam.

Very fluffy Pancakes

BANANA BLUEBERRY LOAF

Tangy and sweet, this fruity loaf is is both tart and sweet. The smooth texture of banana and the delicious flavor of blueberry will be sure to delight. As with the other loafs, this is a lower fat, healthier alternative to most recipes out there.

Recipe Serves	Cook Time
8	90 Minutes

Ingredients	Amount	
Banana	1	Large
Eggs	2	Large
Butter	1	Tablespoon
Sugar	1/3	Cup
Flour	1 1/2	Cups
Greek Yogurt	1/2	Cup
Milk	1/2	Cup
Baking Powder	2	Teaspoons
Salt	1/4	Teaspoon
Blueberries	1 1/2	Cups
Corn Oil	1/4	Tablespoon

Preparation

1. Preheat the oven to 350°F.

2. Crack 2 eggs in a bowl and whisk together. Add the butter and whisk together.

3. Slowly add flour and whisk well.

4. Add the sugar, baking powder, and salt and whisk together with the previous ingredients.

5. Add the greek yogurt & milk and whisk together.

6. In a separate bowl or plate, mash the banana. Then add to the batter.

7. Add the blueberries and slowly mix thoroughly. Either fresh or frozen blueberries can be used, though this recipe recommends frozen blueberries due to their usually sweeter flavor.

8. Add the small amount of corn oil to the baking pan and rub well on bottom, then sprinkle flour.

9. Pour batter in pan and place in oven. Cook for 90 minutes.

Banana Blueberry Loaf

Banana Bread Loaf

Banana bread can be enjoyed any time of day – whether with morning coffee or as dessert, served with ice cream. Best served warm, this banana bread loaf has a beautiful aroma, and tastes accordingly!

Recipe Serves	Cook Time
6	60 Minutes

Ingredients	Amount	
Bananas, Ripe	5	Large
Eggs	1	Large
Sugar	2	Tablespoons
Corn Oil	2	Tablespoons
Flour	1 1/2	Cups
Baking Soda	1	Teaspoon
Baking Powder	1	Teaspoon
Salt	1/2	Teaspoon

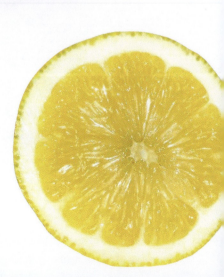

Preparation

1. Preheat the oven to 350°F.

2. Crack the egg in a bowl and whisk well.

3. Add sugar and oil and whisk.

4. In a separate bowl, peel the ripe bananas and mash with a potato masher or other similar utensil. Mash until smooth.

5. Add the flour, baking soda, baking powder, and salt to the eggs, sugar & oil mixture, and whisk thoroughly.

6. Add the mashed bananas and whisk together thoroughly.

Banana Bread Loaf

7. Rub corn oil and then sprinkle flour on the bottom & sides of your baking pan.

8. Pour batter into pan, and place in oven & bake for 55 minutes.

RICE CRISPIES

This classic kids' treat is just as delicious for adults! This recipe takes the classic one we all know & love and adds optional vanilla extract. Served hot or room temperature, these rice crispies are easy and fun to make, and always a treat to have!

Recipe Serves	Cook Time
6	20 Minutes

Ingredients	Amount	
Rice Cereal	1	Cup
Marshmallows	8	Ounces
Butter	1	Tablespoon
Vanilla Extract (optional)	1	Teaspoon

Preparation

1. Melt butter in a non-stick pan over medium heat.

2. When the butter is melted, add the marshmallows, and mix continuously until fully melted.

3. If choosing to add the optional vanilla extract, add a teaspoon when the marshmallows are nearly completely melted, and mix well.

4. Reduce heat to low, add the rice cereal and mix continuously, for 2 minutes.

5. Scoop out rice crispies from pan and place on a serving plate and allow to cool before eating.

RICE CRISPIES

WHITE COFFEE

Not actually coffee, and naturally caffeine free, white coffee is a Mediterranean drink usually enjoyed after a meal or in the evening. White coffee is as clear as water, and naturally slightly bitter. Orange blossom water is the key ingredient to white coffee. This drink is usually enjoyed without sweetener, although according to taste, sugar and/or honey may be added in small amounts, to offset the bitterness and transform this drink into a sweet delight!

Recipe Serves	Preparation Time
2	5 Minutes

Ingredients	Amount	
Water	2	Cups
Orange Blossom Water	2	Tablespoons
Sugar (optional)	1	Teaspoon
Honey (optional, as a sugar alternative)	1	Teaspoon
Mint Leaves (optional)	4	Leaves

Preparation

1. Boil 2 cups of water in a kettle.

2. Pour water in a serving jug.

3. Add room temperature orange blossom water.

4. Optional: add sugar or honey to taste, as well as a few mint leaves.

5. White coffee can be enjoyed either bitter (without sugar / honey) or sweet (with sugar / honey).

White Coffee

Printed in Poland
by Amazon Fulfillment
Poland Sp. z o.o., Wrocław